How Not to Die Hunting in Alaska

Ron Smith

Illustrated by Jeanne Armstrong

To Gibbs!
Enjoy the book and
be careful out there!
Ron Smith

BOOK PUBLISHERS NETWORK

Book Publishers Network
P.O. Box 2256
Bothell • WA • 98041
PH • 425-483-3040
www.bookpublishersnetwork.com

10 9 8 7 6 5 4 3 2 1

Printed in the United States of America

LCCN   2013942752
ISBN   978-1-937454-89-0

Editor: Julie Scandora
Cover design: Laura Zugzda
Interior design: Stephanie Martindale

I dedicate this book to my wife, Marsha,
and to all of my friends who are involved in hunting,
running, and/or creative writing.

Contents

Preface

My wife, Marsha, suggested a title of this book, "How We Almost Died Eighteen Ways." That is a little bit too dramatic for me. Besides, it is an exaggeration. I think there are only fourteen near-death experiences incorporated into these stories. I have told her a million times not to exaggerate. However, in the interests of family harmony, I modified part of her suggestion to "How Not to Die" and simply added "Hunting in Alaska."

There are several reasons to write yet one more book of Alaska hunting stories. First, hunters delight in hearing or reading about the foibles, tight spots, and downright stupidities of other hunters. If you ever did something idiotic in the field, it can be comforting to read about someone else doing something even worse.

A second reason for this book is to indicate that hunting without an ATV or snow machine really is possible. I include stories of walk-in hunts, fly-in hunts, float trips, and of course, a few that were primarily road hunts. I have owned several canoes but never laid out the cash for a riverboat, Skidoo, or four-wheeler. Hunting might have been easier if I had. Certainly, my back would be in better shape if I had.

Third, hunting stories can teach lessons. Making mistakes on hunting trips can be costly, time consuming, or just plain dangerous. I picked stories of hunts during which I learned valuable lessons. As you read these stories, I hope you are entertained, and I suspect you will come away from some of them thinking, "Boy, I don't think I'll do that!" Accordingly, each chapter title indicates one of the lessons I address with particular hunts as examples.

Be safe out there in the field and good luck!

Acknowledgements

First and foremost, I thank my wife, Marsha, for her continuing patience and encouragement. She was a partner on many of the hunts described in this book. Her presence added immeasurably to my enjoyment of them.

Second, thanks to my children, Andy, Hilary, and Jason, all of whom have participated in and/or endured my outdoor and hunting activities.

Without hunting companions, hunting and camping are not as much fun—or exciting! Sharing experiences and stories makes the pilot bread, ramen noodles, and trail mix taste a lot better. I want to thank these hunting partners for enriching my life: Dale Guthrie, A. J. Paul, Paul Matheus, Toos Omtzigt, Russ Shoemaker, Ken Whitten, Owen Guthrie, Oran Paul, Tom Gross, Tom Gillispie, Juli Gillispie, John Fox, John Palmes, Alan Paulson, David Murray, David Klein, Christine Smith, Jim Tucker, Mike McGraugh, Ken Bouwens, Bill Reeburgh, and Judy McDonald.

Over the years, I have had a few hunting companions who were particularly stubborn, less than attentive, or just plain careless. I learned lessons from each of these people, and some of their stories are included in the book. However, rather than using their real names, I simply refer to each of them as "Fred." My apologies to all of the real Freds of the world. I mean no disrespect.

For several years, I have participated in the Fairbanks Summer Arts Festival's creative writing workshop. The workshops, the instructors, and my fellow writers have all inspired me. Thanks to Peggy Shoemaker, Frank Soos, Jeanne Clark, Rob Davidson, and Daryl Farmer for their advice and encouragement.

I appreciate the four people who read and commented on the entire manuscript. Thanks to Marsha Knobel, Mary Lee Guthrie, Mary Zalar, and Jeanne Mars Armstrong. Their comments greatly improved the book.

Thanks to Sheryn Hara, head of Book Publishers Network, for coordinating and managing the production of this book. Julie Scandora edited the entire book, Stephanie Martindale did the page layout, Laura Zugzda created the cover design, and Laura Danforth is handling book distribution.

Last, and certainly not least, my gratitude goes to my friend and cartoonist Jeanne Mars Armstrong. She has captured the spirit and the humor of the stories I told. It was a great pleasure working with her on this project.

1

Think about Water and Lightning

I really should hunt with someone my own size. That thought just popped into my head while clinging to a nearly vertical rock face in the White Mountains with a rifle and fifty-pound pack on my back. The problem: I could not reach the handhold my much taller hunting companion, Dale Guthrie, had just used to reach the top of the slab. My "cling muscles" were tiring, and to make matters worse, we could hear the rumble of thunder heading our way.

"You can reach it, Ron," Dale said.

"No, it is just out of reach," I replied.

"We really need to get off this rock face before that storm hits."

"Dale, I'm stuck here."

Finally, he took some parachute cord from his pack and slid it down to me. "Just tie it onto your pack frame, and I'll pull up enough to relieve some of the weight. Then you can reach the next handhold."

Knot tying usually requires both of my hands. At that moment, both were occupied with clinging. Another thunderclap echoed off the surrounding rocks, and I resolved to tie a knot with one hand. I slid my right hand over to the cord and tried to slip it through the top bar of the pack frame. The effort pushed the frame and me away from the rock. Not good. To keep the pack from moving, I turned my head to the right, gripped the frame with my teeth, and tied the knot. Dale pulled up a little, lightening the load, and I scrambled up the rock.

"Come on; the storm is almost here," he shouted over a deafening clap of thunder. We ran to the top of the ridge, looking for any shelter. As we summited the ridge, the rifle barrel next to my right ear began buzzing. *Zzzt, Zzzt, Zzzt, Zzzt!* A static charge was building on the rifle barrel.

"Run for it, Dale!"

We immediately put down our rifles and packs and got behind the nearest rock. I was imagining the result of lightning striking my rifle with cartridges in the magazine. The nearest bolt hit an outcrop seventy-five yards west of our location. We were spared being fried.

In this particular episode, we got lucky. The first lesson of this chapter is:

Think about lightning.

If you are standing on top of a high ridge in a lightning storm, you don't want a rifle dangling from your shoulder.

This Dall sheep hunt had started the previous morning on a gravel bar far below the ridge. We had unloaded our gear from the Super Cub about noon, assembled our backpacks, and waded across the river. The plan was to traverse the rather wide black-spruce bog, climb the ridge, find a natural spring, and make camp. It was a hot, dry summer, 85°F and sunny, as we started our hike.

We reached the top of the ridge without finding a single puddle, seep, trickle, or mudhole. Nothing. It had been impossible to adhere to one of the cardinal rules of hunting in Alaska: *try not to sweat up your clothes.* I will have more to say about this rule later in the book. We drank most of our water getting to the top so we did not have much choice but to climb back down until we found water. Down we went to a stream on the opposite and steeper side of the ridge. On this hunt, we had consciously thought about water, carried water, and planned for water. But, the weather and terrain conspired against us.

Think about water.

The next morning, we rolled out of the sleeping bags and glassed the ridge top. There were three rams silhouetted on the skyline. We packed camp and started back up the ridge for our encounter with the steep slab, my cling muscles, and the lightning.

After the lightning, sleet, and driving rain subsided, we dried our rifles and carefully crept up to a vantage point. Five rams were grazing about a hundred yards downslope. Two were legal. We could see only their backs and, occasionally, their horns. Patience. All five bedded down. We waited. Ninety minutes later, they all got up and began feeding toward us. At sixty-five yards, they all turned broadside. Dale picked the ram with the broomed horns. That left the smaller ram with slender but intact horns for me. We shot almost simultaneously. Dale's ram went down immediately. Mine staggered ten yards and then fell. The hunting was over. The butchering and the packing were about to begin.

Since we had four days before the plane would come back for us, we had the luxury of moving the meat, heads, and capes nearer the pickup location without having to move our camp in the same load. We established a cache of sheep meat, packed in game bags, high on the mountain but directly above the landing strip. Thus began a few days of mountaintop camping, the most leisurely part of that or any other sheep hunt. We caught up on our sleep, read, and kept an eye on our meat cache. Since caribou season opened the same day as sheep season, we also glassed for caribou. Normally, shooting a caribou on a sheep hunt would not have occurred to either of us. However, we had enough time and a good situation for packing meat down the mountain.

The last afternoon we packed camp, hiked the mile or two to the meat, and added its weight to our backpacks. The total load of camping gear, sheep meat, cape, and head amounted to about 105 pounds each. The traverse down was a challenge. Once we got below the rock and gravel footing of the mountaintop, we encountered spongy moss interspersed with patches of moss-covered rocks. One step was springy and cushioned while the next might be bone-jarring when the moss compressed down to the underlying rock. We got past the hidden rocks and into the bog with its black spruce.

The spongy footing continued through the forest, and we occasionally detoured around fallen trees. Downhill was easier than uphill, but the extra fifty to sixty pounds took its toll. We were pretty tired by the time we reached the landing site. By evening, our camp was reestablished on the gravel bar.

"And now, time for fishing!" I told Dale. We had stashed collapsible rods, reels, and a few lures by the river after we landed. After assembling our tackle, Dale cast into a pool just below a riffle. Instantly a grayling struck. He retrieved a nice, sixteen-inch fish. I cast and quickly caught a fifteen-inch fish. He cast again and caught a fourteen-inch fish.

"Dale, we need to move to the next pool."

We moved downstream, and the sequence from large to not-so-large fish repeated itself. At each pool, we first caught the largest, most dominant fish. That fish was positioned to take the first or best food entering the pool. As the dominant fish was removed from the pool, the second fish in the pecking order took up the best position. We then caught the second fish, and so on.

In the middle of the night, we stopped fishing. By then, we had ten fish to eat and ten fish to pack in the airplane. We built a fire and cooked ourselves a fine grayling dinner.

Think about water.
Throw in a fishing rod for a fly-in hunt.

Water figured prominently in another sheep hunt many years later. Dale, his son Owen, and I were dropped off on a gravel bar in sheep country south of the Brooks Range. From a sheep-hunting point of view, the hunt was a bust. Not only did we not see a single legal ram, but also, rain fell almost continually. After five days, we hiked back to the river and found that our landing strip was not there. It was underwater. The rainy weather we had experienced on the mountaintops had swollen the river.

The plane was due back the next morning so we got out a portable saw and started cutting and pulling willows. Several hours later, we had a useable but short landing strip higher up on the same gravel bar. Since we had no sheep, we did not need a very long strip because the plane would be lightly loaded. We had enough light left to fish, so out came the collapsible rods. After landing several arctic char, we cooked dinner, ate, and turned in. The next morning our pilot landed on the new strip and took us back to civilization. Unfortunately, we had no sheep, but neither did we have a near-death experience to recount.

Of course, crossing streams during a hunt can be treacherous. One solution is to use a light cord or rope to "line" your hunting partner across streams. Using this technique, you anchor yourself upstream from the crossing while your partner holds the rope and wades in. Keep the line taut. Do not tie it to either the pack or the person because, if you fall, your pack will act like an anchor and hold you down on the bottom. As you cross, keep your feet pointed upstream and the force of the moving water will tend to keep your feet on the bottom. Always unhook the waist belt and sternum strap on your backpack because, if you lose your footing, fall, and cannot get out of your straps, you could be trapped in or under your pack.

After the fact, I learned this obvious truth about streams: if you cross a stream on your way in to a hunting location, it is likely that you will have to cross it again on the way out. But, just because it is crossable on the way in does not mean it will be crossable on the way out.

What conditions can cause streams to rise significantly? First, as mentioned above, lots of rain can raise stream levels during the hunt, perhaps making your second crossing of the same stream more hazardous or impossible. Second, if you are hunting near snowfields or glaciers, warm, sunny weather promotes glacial melt and can raise stream levels considerably and quickly.

This second point was demonstrated on another sheep hunt with Dale and his wife, Mary Lee. We easily crossed an ankle-deep stream on the way to a peak in the Wrangell Mountains. On the return, we each had a sheep and a third of camp. The ankle-deep stream had risen about two feet, up to knee level. We got out the rope and lined each other across. As each of us crossed the stream, rooster tails of turbulence formed downstream of each leg. Exciting!

My advice is to remove your pants and put them in the top of your pack. When you get to the other side, you will have something dry to put on. This could be critical in cool or cold weather. However, before you plunge in, put your boots back on your feet. The boulders are too treacherous for bare feet, especially if they are being carried

downstream by the current. Also, your feet often go numb and lose any dexterity they might have had when they were warm.

Water played an integral role in another sheep hunt. This hunt took place above a tributary of the Yukon near Eagle. Dale, George Frison, and I were dropped on a gravel bar of the tributary intending to hunt the high ridges to the north. We headed up a narrow stream channel identified on the map as Funnel Creek. The bed was eight feet wide with vertical sidewalls maybe ten feet high in places. Above the sidewalls, the slope moderated a bit, consisting of boulders covered with a thin veneer of moss and an occasional piece of driftwood. Looking up the creek, I understood the origin of the name Funnel Creek: the vertical profile looked like a funnel. At least I thought that was the origin.

The next day involved a long climb to sheep country in glorious sunshine and a climb onto another vertical face upon which I lost my bejeebers … scared them right out of me! Maybe I should mention that I am afraid of heights.

We dropped our gear near the summit of the ridge and began glassing. Shortly, we spotted a ram down in the spruce trees. George decided to set up camp while Dale and I headed down the ridge to try for the sheep. To get a vantage, we climbed onto another pinnacle that scared both of us. Late in the afternoon, the ram came sneaking out of a spruce thicket, and Dale put him down with one shot.

Before the day ended, the weather went completely sour. We packed the sheep to camp in driving wind and rain. The next four days were spent in the tent hoping for a change. Finally, we broke camp in the rain and headed back the way we came.

Funnel Creek was a raging torrent at least eight feet deep. It looked like a giant, industrial-strength toilet being flushed. I now understood the presence of driftwood pieces ten feet above the bottom of the creek. They had been deposited during an even bigger runoff. We walked along the hillsides on the slippery boulders and took several falls each. Rain gear was useless because, even if it were totally waterproof, it could not breathe fast enough to dispel the moisture from our sweating. We were all soaked to the bone.

We arrived at the tributary and immediately gathered dead spruce branches from live trees for a fire. The powdery beard lichen that hangs from spruce branches burns even when somewhat damp. Soon we had enough fire to dry additional firewood. Standing near the roaring fire, we radiated steam from every square inch of our clothing.

I feel compelled to say a little more about raingear. There are several types, each with its advantages. First, there is the lightweight, breathable raingear with Gore-Tex or a similar membrane that allows perspiration to move through the fabric to the outside. This stuff is expensive, and I have found there are conditions where it fails. In torrential rain, a person carrying a heavy load just is not going to stay dry.

The opposite approach is to wear heavy, rubberized impervious gear like Helly Hansens. Not quite as expensive, but rainwater does not come through. Sweat does not escape either.

Lightweight, polypropylene shells are a third alternative. These are less expensive, usually, than either of the above alternatives. They are also less durable and, if you try hard, can be ripped.

Perhaps as important as material is the length of the raincoat. I have been on hunts during which I wore hip waders and a raincoat. If the raincoat is too short, all the rainwater runs into your waders.

So, you need to think about how active you will be, how much rain you might get, and how much money you want to spend on raingear. If you go too cheap on raingear for a hunt, you might not live to enjoy the savings.

Bottom line: *think about water*. Plan ahead for the possibility of high-water events along your hiking route. Think about alternate routes if streams or rivers rise. Have good rain gear and pay attention to scour marks and flotsam lodged high above the streambed. And, do not forget: *think about lightning!*

2

Don't Overestimate Your Transportation

In early spring, caribou begin to move away from winter range in the boreal forest and head for higher ground. Females will drop their calves (and antlers) on high, wind-swept ridges, relatively free of insects and where they can see predators coming a long way away. As an example, the Nelchina herd spends the winter east of the Richardson Highway in the upper Copper River drainages and crosses the Richardson singly or in small groups in March and April. Snowshoe hare season in interior Alaska never closes, and ptarmigan season coincides, more or less, with caribou season. Therefore, back in the 1970s, this migration provided the opportunity for springtime mixed-bag hunting for both road hunters and snow-machine hunters.

In March 1971, Dale Guthrie and I headed down the road with two graduate students, John Palmes and Al Paulson. We intended to hunt for caribou, snowshoe hares, and ptarmigan. Populations of hares and ptarmigan were relatively high in 1971, and graduate students (and biology faculty) will eat anything, so we were all in good spirits. The four of us, plus coats, rifles, snowshoes, food, and sleeping bags, were packed into my 1968 Bronco. We planned to stay overnight in the bunkhouse at Sourdough Lodge: down on Friday afternoon, back on Saturday afternoon, a twenty-four-hour hunt.

At Donnelly Dome, just south of Delta Junction, we saw hares along the road. John and Al got four. We stuffed them behind the rear bench seat and continued on to Summit Lake. There were lots of ptarmigan on the slopes along the north shore of the lake. All four of us piled out and hunted ptarmigan. In an hour, we had sixty birds. With a twenty-bird limit per person, we were still under our group limit. We managed to fit them all under the rear seat.

Thirty miles later, well past Paxson, we had not seen any caribou. An old trail, completely snowed-in, intersected the highway, heading east through the spruce/aspen forest. There were many hare tracks so we strapped on our snowshoes and moved down the trail carrying .22 rifles for the hares and larger caliber rifles for any caribou that we might find.

There were lots of hares. Each hare we got was carried to the trail and left for our walk back to the highway. Still no caribou. However, we had so many hares we had to tie their legs together in stringers and drag them back to the road. Counting them as we stuffed them under, behind, and beside that rear seat, we discovered we had added fifty-seven hares to our bag. With no closed season and no bag limit on hares in the interior, a hunter can really load up on hare meat. The back seat was getting decidedly cramped.

As we finished loading the hares, two other road hunters cruised by in a 1970 Cadillac, a real battleship. We had met them on the road several times already. They nodded and drove on, looking for caribou. By now, it was time for us to head down the road to Sourdough. We had an hour of daylight left.

Rounding a curve in the road, we saw a caribou cross the road a hundred yards ahead. I pulled over, and we all jumped out. Before we could load rifles and wade off the road right-of-way, five more animals had crossed. There was a lot of excitement, especially for Al and John, neither of whom had gotten caribou before. We got all six. The limit was three caribou per person back then. I have thanked my lucky stars many times that there were only six. Legally, we could have bagged up to twelve.

We quickly gutted the caribou and dragged them to the road. Coincidentally, the Cadillac guys reappeared and slid down the power window, *zzzzzt*, and asked, "How many were there?"

"Six," I replied.

"How many did you get?"

"Six." *Zzzzzt*, and away they went, completely disgusted with us. We never saw them again.

At this point, it finally occurred to us that we might have a problem hauling all of these animals home. Clearly, the back half of the Bronco was fully occupied with two hunters, gear, sixty ptarmigan, and sixty-one hares. There was nothing for it but to put the six caribou on top. It seemed like a good idea at the time. Initially, everything rode well. However, after a few bumps in the road, the interior of the Bronco's top looked like a mine disaster as the roof had crumpled under the weight of the overburden. Al and John were trying to hold up the roof long enough for us to get to Sourdough.

We drove in to the roadhouse, bought burgers, and pitched into the bunkhouse. The next morning over breakfast, we decided that since the vehicle looked like a mine cave-in we should treat it like one. Lying around the roadhouse were pieces of lumber left over from building nearby bridges and buildings. We borrowed a handsaw and set to work cutting four-by-fours and heavy planking. We pulled the caribou off the roof, shored up the inside, and piled the animals back on. Now the inside of the vehicle looked like a macabre mine shaft. We successfully returned to Fairbanks with all of our animals on board. However, I learned:

Don't overestimate your transportation.

Examples of overestimating the capabilities of Super Cubs, snow machines, and Cessna 185s are numerous in Alaska. Fortunately, I cannot relate any such stories from my own experience. However, I do have an excellent example of overestimating the capacity of a canoe.

The canoe example unfolded on a moose hunt in lower Tangle Lakes. Dale, Russ Shoemaker, and I drove down to Tangle Lakes from Fairbanks on a Friday afternoon, put the canoe in the water, and loaded our gear. Our transportation was a seventeen-foot fiberglass canoe molded around a Grumman aluminum model. There were lots of layers of fabric and glass, and it weighed ninety pounds. We headed across the lake and down the outlet stream. The passage down from the upper Tangle Lake consists of an outlet stream, with rapids, leading to a second lake. This second lake is, in turn, separated from a third lake by more stream and more rapids. The first stretch of rapids was easy, and we reached the second lake with plenty of daylight left to set up camp. The next morning, we spotted a legal moose on the hillside opposite our camp. Canoeing across, we made the stalk successfully, skinned, gutted, and quartered the animal, and started packing.

It was a medium-sized moose, cut into only five pieces. The brain of the bunch insisted we not bone out the meat. Therefore, the hindquarters weighed 125 pounds each, the neck meat was eighty to ninety pounds, and the front shoulders were a whopping 145 pounds each. Each of these five pieces constituted a full load. If I had known these facts at the time, I would never have packed the shoulder! I weighed 155 pounds, so 94 percent of my body weight, the moose shoulder, added to my body weight was too much. Fortunately, we only had to pack the loads a half-mile back to the lake. With that much weight, I needed both Russ and Dale to help me get on my feet. At one point, following the other two, I stepped in mud and got my boot stuck. Balancing the pack and trying to pull my foot out of the mud was almost impossible. I had to call for help. If I had lost my balance, my leg would have snapped like a twig.

Don't overestimate your transportation, especially if YOU are the transportation!

Back down on the lake, we rested, had a snack, and went back to glassing. Two moose ran down the ridge and crossed the lake downstream from us. Another party of hunters shot the cow; the young bull ran on. Back then, there was an overlap of two days in the bull and cow seasons in the Alaska Range. Eventually the bull climbed the ridge opposite us and came into view. I jumped in the canoe and paddled across. While I climbed, Dale and Russ gave me hand signals toward the moose. I got it down and started the gutting and skinning.

Since Russ and Dale were on the wrong side of the lake without a canoe and since it turned out the other hunters could not find their moose, Dale worked out a trade: a ride across the lake in their canoe in exchange for help in locating their dead moose. The other hunting party agreed and transported Russ and Dale. Dale quickly found their moose. When they caught up to me, my bull was ready to transport … in smaller pieces than the first moose because it was a smaller moose.

Sunday morning dawned, and we broke camp. We piled the moose pieces in the middle of the canoe and our gear around the two paddling positions, fore and aft. With Russ sprawled across the meat pile, we paddled up the lake. When we reached the rapids, we attached a rope to the bow and started pulling the load upstream. The canoe occasionally scraped rocks as we progressed. By mid-afternoon, we reached the main lake.

All we had to do was paddle across the lake back to the carryall. A steady breeze was blowing, and we should have hugged the lee shore all the way around the lake. Instead, we elected to head straight across.

Of course, when we got to the middle, the wind picked up. Occasionally the chop washed over the gunwales.

Russ began to bail water with a cooking pot. Very quickly, we were barely afloat. Dale and I paddled with total abandon while Russ bailed as if his life depended upon it. It did. As we neared shore, I was sure we had it made … but I was wrong. The canoe sank about five feet from the boat launch. Russ started the vehicle and got the heater blasting while Dale and I started retrieving gear, rifles, and moose meat. It took a while, but we got everything.

When we lifted the canoe over our heads to put it on the roof rack, we could see daylight through a dozen holes in the bottom. There was simply too much weight in the canoe. The only reason we did not sink in the middle of the lake was that, most of the time, the moose hams were pressing down on most of the holes. *Don't overestimate your transportation.*

Would you believe I had a chance to repeat the "1968 Bronco caribou hunt" the following year? Of course, I realized the drawbacks (my wife calls them mistakes) of the previous episode and thought seriously about the remedies. First, I unbolted and removed the back seat. With no back seat, I had to limit the size of the hunting party to two: Bill Reeburgh and myself. Since I was not planning to stack caribou on the roof, we tied an akio up there instead. An akio is a heavy fiberglass sled on wooden runners. At ten feet in length, it looks like a banana-split dish on steroids.

Friday afternoon after classes (we both taught at the university in Fairbanks), Bill and I headed to Paxson. In mid-November, daylight lasts only about five hours. The plan was to stay at Paxson Lodge and hunt the Denali Highway on Saturday. We were up before dawn, not

much of an accomplishment when sun-up is at 10:00 AM. Temperatures were moderate, 0°F to -10°F, but the wind was blowing hard. As the Bronco climbed toward the tundra, we were breaking through drifts, hoping the road would not close behind us.

A band of eight caribou crossed the road well ahead of us. I stopped the Bronco, and we gathered our packs, rifles, and snowshoes and hiked after them. We moved fast, trying to catch up to the band and, shortly, overtook the trailing bull. Lying down behind a drift, we both aimed and shot. The bull went down, fortunately for us. We had shot directly into the wind. The muzzle blast had dislodged ice crystals from the drift, causing the wind to drive them back into our faces. It felt like being stuck repeatedly with toothpicks. We were unenthusiastic about shooting into the wind again.

After quickly gutting the bull, we followed the rest of the band. A half-mile later, we caught up to them. They were feeding in a swale, out of the wind. We again laid our packs on a snowdrift and shot. This time, the wind was to our backs. Very quickly, we had five more caribou down. Like the previous year, each resident hunter had a three-caribou limit.

These five were lying close together so I switched to a cheap pair of gloves and started gutting. As I finished one, I would walk the short distance to the next, and my bloody gloves would freeze solid. Cutting into the next would thaw them; walking to the next animal would refreeze them. I was frostbiting my fingers. Although I still have all ten digits, I have suffered cold hands and poor circulation ever since.

Keep your warm gloves or mitts on!

By the time we got back to the Bronco, it was almost dark. We drove closer to the five animals, dragged them to the tailgate, and loaded them. Back to the Paxson Lodge and another night in a warm bed. What a bunch of softies!

Sunday morning, we returned for the last animal, the bull we had first shot. The akio worked great on the packed snow. In twenty minutes, we were back to the vehicle with the animal. The plan was to shove this last animal in back with the other five. Just push them aside and squeeze it in, right? Wrong!

The five animals inside were frozen solid in a variety of contorted positions. The last animal was, not surprisingly, frozen too. No way would that last one fit inside. And, no way would I put a caribou back up on the roof of the Bronco. I had a clear picture in my mind of 250 miles of bouncing over a frozen road and the resulting "mine disaster" scene I would have, again, with the vehicle. So, we tied the last one to the grill. It was not cheap exhibitionism. It was the only option I could think of with a completely frozen caribou. Again, *don't overestimate your transportation*. And, for heaven's sake, do not overestimate twice with the same vehicle!

3

Don't Tip over the Canoe

Once, years ago, I was solo moose hunting on the wrong side of the Chena River, near Fairbanks. That is, I had crossed the river by bridge and then hiked far downriver. To return the way I had come would have involved fighting through miles of brush or a long detour. Instead, I decided to wade across the river, get on the Chena Hot Springs Road, and hike back to my truck. It was cold and windy that day, and I did not relish getting totally wet in the river. So, I decided to peel off my Carhartts and stuff them in my backpack. At least I would have something dry on my legs for the rest of the hike. I do not take my pants off every time I get near water. However, it seemed like a good idea at the time.

I grabbed the bough of a spruce growing on the bank and eased myself in. I was knee deep when I heard a thump that sounded exactly like a paddle hitting the side of a canoe. I looked upstream, past the spruce, and saw an aluminum canoe bearing down on me, propelled by two women. There was no time to retreat into the willows so I froze where I was, hoping that my camouflage raincoat would suffice. The ladies in the canoe passed within three feet of me and never glanced my direction. I do not know if that fact was a testament to their focus on paddling or to the effectiveness of my camouflage. It does not really matter. The important thing is that they did not see a half-naked man in the wilderness and, consequently, they did not tip over their canoe.

I have wondered how receptive they might have been to being rescued under those circumstances. I might have gotten a paddling. In any case:

Don't tip over your canoe,
even when startled.

I know a few things about canoeing, but I am no expert. I know the person in the back can turn the canoe, often in spite of the efforts of the paddler in front. The basic J-stroke from the rear of the canoe can be modified to turn left, right, or continue straight ahead. The paddler in front can simply provide energy for forward motion or, preferably, assist in steering by employing pull-strokes and push-strokes as appropriate. When running rapids, the paddler in front shouts steering directions to the rear paddler and employs pull- or push-strokes to avoid boulders or sweepers. The more experience two canoeists have working together, the less likely they are to tip over the canoe.

If you know the J-stroke, you can always paddle from the same side of the canoe. If you do not have to switch the paddle from one side of the canoe to the other, you don't dribble as much water into the canoe. Try to avoid dribbling water into the canoe.

Early in my canoeing history, I took a date for a romantic ride across a lake. We were in a fourteen-foot "rat" canoe, a lightweight canoe favored by springtime muskrat hunters. Such a canoe can easily be dragged from one ice-free pond to another. And, it can easily be paddled solo.

The young woman was not interested in paddling so she sat in the middle of the canoe, right in front of me. The first time I switched the paddle from one side to the other, a short stream of droplets cascaded off the paddle onto the back of her neck. I cannot think of anything that chills a romance faster than ice water down a woman's neck. That

very night, alone, I picked up a book on canoeing and learned about the J-stroke.

Dale Guthrie and I have worked together in canoes for a long time and have not had any mishaps for years. Early on, when he was teaching me the basics, we were floating the lower Chena. He decided I needed to know how to back the canoe upstream.

"All we have to do, Ron, is a reverse stroke, both of us simultaneously. But, put some energy into it. Ready? Now!"

From the front of the canoe, I did a powerful reverse stroke. We were in the water faster than you could count "One!"

"It didn't work, Dale. We're still drifting downstream, and we're not in the canoe!"

The mistake we made was this: we were both paddling on the same side of the boat. One powerful stroke and we rolled over. To date, that is the only time I have completely dumped a canoe.

Years later, I was navigating a piece of the upper Chena River with our friends, Richard and Cheryl Scott, their six-year-old boy, Garrett, and my son, Jason. Cheryl was in the front seat of our seventeen-foot plastic canoe, giving directions and keeping us out of the sweepers. I was in back. We spotted a nice gravel bar for a picnic and started maneuvering for a landing. I did a braking move that was a little too vigorous, and the canoe tipped far enough to allow some water to flow over one gunwale. We built a fire to dry our butts and all was well.

It is good to know your canoe and how vigorously to respond to a variety of situations. *Don't tip over your canoe.*

For several years, Dale and I spent opening mornings of waterfowl season pass-shooting ducks in Goldstream Valley, near Fairbanks. The evening before the opener, we'd drag a canoe into a pond, hide it, and set out some decoys. One year, I decided to hunt moose elsewhere instead of ducks at our usual location. Dale and his son, Owen, plus their chocolate Lab, Pete, went after the ducks. By mid-afternoon, I had given up on moose and was back home calling Dale to get a report on the duck hunt.

Mary Lee, Dale's wife, answered the phone and said, "Dale's not here right now. He went to town to rent a magnet."

"Uh-oh! Dumped the canoe, did he?" I asked.

She answered, "I'll let him tell you."

Dale, Owen, and Pete were all in the canoe when a small flock of widgeons flew past. Owen shot, and a duck dropped into the pond. Pete launched himself into the water, and the canoe capsized. In the excitement that followed, two shotguns went to the bottom. The magnet would be used to grapple for the shotguns. Both Dale and Owen were shooting old, sixties-vintage Remingtons with heavy steel receivers, something the magnet could latch onto. The magnet worked.

Even though Dale had retrieved their shotguns, he was not feeling lucky. I pointed out that he could have been using his favorite shotgun, a Winchester Model 59, also from the early sixties. This shotgun, ahead of its time, has an aluminum alloy receiver and a fiberglass barrel. The magnet would have totally ignored the Model 59. My advice is: *don't tip over your canoe.* And, don't let your dog tip over the canoe. Remaining upright is a lot simpler than going for a magnet or diving for your guns.

You can get really wet in a canoe without resorting to actually tipping it over. One way is to overload the canoe until you have little or no freeboard. Freeboard is the vertical distance from the water surface to the top of the gunwale. The more weight you load on a canoe, the lower the freeboard.

I found that, with very little freeboard, I needed to watch out for two things. The first is fidgeting. Wiggling around in the seat can easily rock the canoe enough to take on water. Several times, we have taken on water while pass-shooting ducks on interior ponds. Raising a shotgun and getting it on the bird is often a sudden movement that tips the canoe. Swinging on a passing duck, to a canoe, is the same as fidgeting.

The second thing that you need to watch out for is waves or "chop." You might get by with two inches of freeboard in perfectly calm water. But, add a little wind and three-inch waves, and your canoe will take on water.

Even if you do not overload the canoe, you can still get very wet. A lightly loaded canoe can fill with water. All you have to do is poke a hole in the bottom! Refer to the last chapter for an excellent example of such foolishness.

One of the more desperate and comic examples of the strategy of poking a hole in a boat was observed by my friend, A. J. Paul. He was standing on the dock in Seward, Alaska, watching a fisherman in a small aluminum skiff some distance offshore pull a large halibut on board. The fish began thrashing violently, and the man attempted to dispatch it with a .410 shotgun. Unfortunately, he missed the halibut and blew a hole in the bottom of his boat. A.J. said he had never seen anyone row that hard before.

My most ill-starred sheep hunt involved a canoe. Russ Shoemaker, who knew nothing about canoes, and I, who knew slightly more, decided to hunt sheep along the flanks of Black Rapids Glacier in the Alaska Range. I borrowed a canvas canoe from a friend. We loaded the canoe and our gear and drove down the Richardson Highway, arriving at Black Rapids in late afternoon. After carefully placing all of our stuff in the canoe, we surveyed the river. Below the glacier, the river was braided into five channels. Above the glacier, the entire Delta River swept through a single channel with a series of standing waves. Risk the river in five, shallow channels or in a single, deep, nasty channel with standing waves? We chose the single channel. Idiots!

We pushed away from the bank, and with two strokes, we were in the middle of the standing waves.

Russ looked at the waves and exclaimed, "Geez!"

I answered, "Just a few more strokes and we're across, Russ."

As the bow of the canoe encountered the slower-moving water near shore, it slowed, allowing the stern to swing around. The starboard side of the canoe, now parallel with the shore, gently bumped the beach. We stepped out completely dry. It could have been Divine Providence or the Great Good Luck of the Stupid. We didn't care but vowed to face the five braided channels on the return rather than revisit the standing waves.

Other than the near-disaster with the canoe, the rest of the hunt was filled with ineptitude and miscommunications. First, our packs were too heavy by far. Mine was loaded with canned stew, and Russ had an entire six-pack of Tab, a disgusting diet cola that neither of us liked. Tab is a beverage that Dale could drink because it did not have sugar and, therefore, did not cause his blood glucose to bottom out.

Russ did not realize that on previous hunts Dale drank the Tab, not me. So, a lot of extra weight for something we did not want to drink. Then, there was the episode of walking on the skyline while stalking a ram. That did not turn out well unless you enjoy watching a legal sheep rapidly leaving the country. We hunted hard but foolishly. Neither of us got a sheep.

Finally, blessedly, our allotted days for sheep hunting lapsed. We did not even come close to getting a sheep. We hiked back down to the Delta River and put the canoe in the water. Once it was loaded, we pushed off across the first braid. This first passage was uneventful, except for a little scraping on the gravel stream bottom. The other four braids were a repeat of the first.

The canoe shot out of the last riffle into deeper water, only a hundred yards to the pickup. We had it made … except for the water accumulating in the bottom of the canoe. We had neither splashed with the paddles nor tipped the canoe. The only other source of water had to be through the bottom of the canoe!

The canoe sank just as we were about to step onto shore. We spent a while, up to our waists, pulling very wet gear out of the river. The ride home was pretty chilly until the truck heater dried us out. We spent a lot of time the following spring repairing that canoe.

Don't scrape holes in the bottom of the canoe!

One would think that, having done this once, an intelligent person would not repeat the mistake. But, if you have read this far, you already know that some of us need to learn a lesson more than once.

I have a few more thoughts on canoeing. I have never been one to horse around in a canoe, but I know people who do. Once I watched several people in two canoes try to splash each other with their paddles. The canoes were coasting downstream broadside to each other. Paddles were being employed first to "spank" water in the direction of the other canoe. Then, one man decided to use the paddle like a shovel, hoping to move a lot of water into his opponent's boat. Instead, his forceful upward stroke simply caused his own canoe to roll over. Poetic justice.

Engaging in any activity that might startle your canoe-mate can result in fidgeting and/or wiggling that can tip your canoe. So, for instance, do not get cute and purposely dribble water down the neck of your fellow canoeist. In my own unintentional incident, long ago, I got lucky. The young lady didn't thrash around. She simply went rigid. Rigid and frigid at least did not capsize the canoe … just our budding relationship.

4

Try Not to Sweat

I do not remember why I did not have an extra raincoat or windbreaker with me. Dad and I were, otherwise, pretty well equipped for an early fall hunt in the high country. He, Russ Shoemaker, and I were after caribou and ptarmigan in the Tanana Uplands on a windy, cloudy, late August day.

I told Dad that once we started walking, his chamois shirt, down vest, and jacket would be more than enough to keep him warm.

"Any more and you'll get all sweaty, Dad."

"I don't care; I don't want that wind on me," he answered. All we had were some thirty-gallon garbage bags so I cut three holes in one of them: one hole for his head and two more for his arms. We pulled it over him and got his arms through. "That's better. Let's go," he said.

After hours of hiking across the tundra, we returned to the truck. Poor Dad was stewed in his own perspiration inside that non-breathable "garment." All he could say was "Get me out of this infernal bag!" Russ and I ripped the bag off him, and Dad got chilled right away. We started the truck, got the heater going, and eventually, got Dad dried out.

Of course, sweating is a mechanism to rid us of excess body heat. Sweat is transformed from liquid to water vapor on the skin in a heat-consuming change of phase. This is evaporative cooling.

While hiking or hunting, it is useful to keep sweating to a minimum. Why? First, when you are sweating, you are losing lots of water that has to be replaced by drinking. Do you have a water bottle in your pack? How about water purification? Both are essential, especially so when sweating.

Second, as the sweat evaporates from your skin, you lose body heat, whether you want to or not. Assume you are backpacking in a cool wind, your clothes get sweaty, you get tired and stop for a rest. The wind will chill you much more rapidly than if you were dry.

Third, some clothing loses its insulative value when wet. Every outdoors person needs to do the research on synthetic fiber clothing and layering. Perhaps most important, one needs to pace oneself.

Years ago, I got an excellent chance to explain the layering and pacing to a new hunting companion. He was a new arrival to Alaska. He had hunted in Arizona but knew nothing about what to do in Alaska. Normally, I would not have taken him hunting. I knew little about him, and I am pretty careful about picking hunting partners. However, our wives worked closely together professionally, and my wife exerted pressure on me to take this guy hunting. OK, we'll go hunting. Mistake.

I gave Fred (that was not really his name) an equipment list for a two-day hunt. On the way up the road, I explained that it was good to hike at a pace at which we would not sweat. We could adjust heat loss by putting on or removing vests, jackets, shirts, hats, and gloves.

We arrived at our jumping-off point, packed our backpacks, and started hiking. Fred took off like a jackrabbit. I told him to slow down.

He said, "This is my normal walking pace; I can't be crawling along at a snail's pace."

"You'll get all sweaty, and besides, how are you going to spot any game walking that fast?

He countered: "It's a nice day. Who cares if we get sweaty?"

After several hours of nonproductive, fast walking, I decided we needed to get on the highest point in the vicinity for a better vantage in glassing. Of course, the highest point was the windiest point. I sat down and immediately put on my windbreaker, hat, and gloves. My companion was shivering in a few minutes.

"Put on your windbreaker," I told him.

"Didn't bring it," he answered.

"Put on your hat and gloves," I suggested.

"Didn't bring them either," he responded.

"Didn't I tell you to bring that stuff?"

"Yeah, but it was a sunny day when we started walking, and I didn't think I'd need it."

I asked, "Have you always been a slow learner?"

Try not to sweat.
If you do, put on a jacket!

I recall another hunt in which sweating became an issue. It was the last day of moose season, 1971. Russ Shoemaker and I were glassing from a very high vantage point on a dome near Fairbanks and spotted two moose down near the bottom of a canyon, perhaps two miles away. Rather than exercising good judgment, we went after them and got both.

After a quick lunch, we butchered them and loaded about eighty pounds in each of our packs. Instead of turning around and going back the way we had come, we decided to take a different route. We were trying to avoid at least a mile of fallen trees left over from an old burn. The plan was to go down the canyon, climb a low ridge, and follow it back to the road. It seemed like a good idea at the time.

Bushwhacking down the canyon was bad. Climbing the low ridge was much worse. During a rest break, we finished off our food. We discovered that our recollection of the "low ridge" was seriously flawed. Looking at maps afterward, we found that it was five miles long and intersected the road four miles from our vehicle. It turned out to be a nine- or ten-mile walk instead of a two-mile climb back the way we had gone in. Brilliant.

It was midnight when we got back to the road. We were exhausted, out of food, and had sweated through our jackets. We left the packs and started up the road. Shortly, I completely ran out of steam.

"Russ, I'm going to lie down for a few minutes."

"I'll go get the car and come back for you, Ron."

I lay down on my back in the middle of the road. The temperature was near zero, and there was a packed layer of snow on the road. Soon, I began to shiver. It was time to get up and get moving again. I tried to roll over onto my hands and knees but I could not move. My jacket was frozen to the road.

Try not to sweat.
But if you do, *don't lie down in the middle of a frozen road!*

Now what? Hypothermia was creeping up on me, and I thought seriously of just remaining where I was. It was not going to be a painful death. I was beginning to relax when I heard a vehicle coming. It was not Russ. It was coming from the other direction.

Hypothermia might be a painless way to die, but getting run over was not going to be painless. I unzipped my jacket and rolled over. Grabbing my jacket collar, I stood up and gave a mighty pull. The outer layer of fabric plus some of the insulation remained on the road.

Donning the remnants of the coat, I stumbled up the road. In appearance and behavior, I could have easily been mistaken for a down-and-out drunk from downtown Fairbanks. Headlights loomed in front of me. I flagged down the driver. He gave me a lift to our vehicle. The hot air in the cab of that pickup was, quite literally, a life-saver.

Thanking the driver profusely, I climbed out. Before I could slam the door, he asked, "What happened to your coat?"

"The truth? It was frozen to the road with me in it."

"No, man. I think you are drunk!" he replied.

Russ was inside his carryall warming it up. He did not notice my coat. We ate some candy bars we had left in the vehicle and headed toward home. When we reached my coat fragment in the road, Russ asked, "What was that thing in the road?"

"Roadkill coat."

"What?"

"Never mind, Russ."

We went back the next day with two more packers and retrieved the rest of the meat. We hiked the short way out that time. It is almost impossible to pack moose meat without sweating but *try not to sweat*. And, for heaven's sake, *don't lie down in the middle of a frozen road*. Also, study the maps of your hunting area thoroughly.

5

Which Way Is the Wind Blowing?

Virtually every hunter in North America pays attention to which way the wind is blowing. Human scent almost always spooks game animals. This fact has led to the development of a ton of outdoor products, such as clothing that mostly locks in your scent and detergents and sprays that eliminate human scent from clothing. I am not very knowledgeable about these products. I simply fall back on noting wind direction and, when appropriate, hunting upwind. In spite of an awareness of wind direction, a hunter can easily run afoul of shifting wind. I vividly recall such an episode.

It was one of the low points in my hunting career. I had recently sold several rifles to pay bills and had only two left. One was an old Savage lever action in a .250 Savage caliber. With its 7.5 power scope, it was a great caribou rifle. I also had used it successfully on a large black bear and a bull moose.

All of my hunting partners were either out of town or out of state so I hunted alone. I drove down to the Denali Highway, tented the night, and hiked into the mountains the next morning. The morning passed with no caribou to be found. Dall sheep crossed below me several times, but I saw no legal rams. In mid-afternoon, I spotted a beautiful silvertip grizzly, checked the wind, and headed toward it.

As I drew nearer the bear, my adrenaline levels were pretty high. Or, was I hearing an inner scream? After all, the .250 Savage is not grizzly medicine, and I had no backup, neither extra rifle nor armed hunting partner. I figured I would approach from downwind and get close enough for a headshot. Lots of crawling got me within forty yards of the bear. I set up a prone shot using my pack as a rest. The grizzly's head almost filled the field of view in the scope. I started a slow, deliberate squeeze on the trigger. Just before I expected the rifle to discharge, a second grizzly head intruded on my sight picture. Not good. I had to be looking at the heads of a sow and her almost fully-grown cub. The good news was: I had not shot. The bad news was: the sow stood on her hind legs, turning her head side-to-side sniffing. The wind was shifting around, and she was occasionally getting my scent. I had paid attention to the wind, but it was now starting to blow erratically. Again the wind shifted, and the sow returned to feeding. When the heads of both the sow and her offspring were down, I crawled backward. When one or the other bear stood on hind legs, I froze. My inner scream was at full volume, and I was, belatedly, giving it my full attention. Fifteen minutes later, I was a safe distance away. During that fifteen minutes, the sow and/or cub had stood and tested the wind at least a dozen times.

Pay attention to wind direction.

Another wind-related event involved moose vocalizations. The last evening of moose season, I was glassing a ridge at tree line. There was not a moose in sight. Suddenly, I heard a loud moaning sound. To a human, it could have been a very unhappy, perhaps inebriated woman giving voice to her frustrations. In reality, it was a cow moose calling. Almost immediately, a cow and calf moved out of a huge willow and alder patch. Shortly, a bull emanated from the same patch. All three moved downslope toward thick cover.

I did my best rendition of a bull grunt, and the bull stopped. Too far away for a shot, I headed toward the bull. Every time he moved to follow the cow, I grunted. Every time I grunted, the bull stopped and faced my direction. At about two hundred yards, the bull abandoned the cow altogether and started walking in the opposite direction. That course would take him directly downwind of me. Just before he reached that position, he was moving broadside and came clear of the brush. That was his undoing. He was mine.

I am convinced that the bull was heading downwind to get a whiff of what he thought was a challenging bull. Bulls in rut have really stinky urine. They urinate on their hind legs and wallow in their own urine. The odor has an effect on females but can probably be evaluated by other males as well.

Pay attention to wind direction.
And learn the sounds that attract bull moose.

Several years later, I had an opportunity to put the sounds and the wind direction together successfully in another moose hunt. Ken Bouwens and I went down in the Goldstream flats, near Fairbanks, to hunt moose. He wanted me to call. I used, successively, the cow moan, antler thrashing, and bull grunts. Nothing showed up, but Ken thought I sounded authentic enough to take me to his real hunting spot, miles away.

The next evening, we drove out to an old, overgrown clear-cut. I asked Ken to move about forty yards downwind. If a bull came to the calling, I was sure he would try to check scent. An hour of cow moans produced nothing. When I followed the last moan with brush thrashing, there was an immediate response: brush thrashing followed by a bull grunt. In the next ten minutes, the bull grunted every ten to fifteen seconds, steadily moving closer. I kept responding. At last, he circled downwind, stepping out of the brush about twenty-five yards from Ken. One shot. Lights out. *Learn the sounds that attract bull moose.*

I have several other moose-calling incidents, one of which produced totally unexpected results. Paul Matheus, his wife Toos Omtzigt, and I planned a hike/hunt for opening day of moose season. We would start above tree line and walk down a five-mile ridge to a logging road. We stashed a vehicle on the logging road the night before and had my wife, Marsha, drop us off on top.

Except for the early morning clouds on the tops of the ridges, it was a perfect day, cool and sunny. Down we went, seeing lots of moose sign. About halfway down the ridge, Paul found some particularly fresh droppings and tracks. He and Toos decided to follow the tracks; I would slowly continue downhill. We planned to meet in fifteen minutes.

I eased down the ridge very slowly, listening for them to return. After forty-five minutes and no sign of them, I began to wonder if they were ahead of me. But, maybe they were behind me … What to do? My solution was to continue downward but to let them know where I was. I started moaning, repeating the cow vocalization every five minutes, way too often to be a real cow moose.

Finally, I heard them crashing through the woods in my direction. My relief turned to astonishment when a young bull moose emerged from the thicket instead of Paul and Toos. A quick calculation told me it was about a mile and a half to the truck and that it was a small bull. He stopped broadside at thirty-five yards. I shot, and the moose staggered. I put another round into the lungs, but the bull just stood there. Finally, I put a third shot in the neck, right behind the ear. That did it. The moose had come crosswind to get to me. *Learn the sounds that attract bulls* and *pay attention to wind direction.*

Paul and Toos were attracted by the rifle shots. *Learn the sounds that attract your hunting companions.* We butchered the bull, got the meat in game bags, and headed downslope. Each of us had a load of meat. It was way after dark when we stumbled onto the logging road and found the truck. The next day, we went back with two more packers, Ken Bouwens and Nancy Greiner, and finished the job by mid-day.

Here is one last, ridiculous example in which I could have used wind direction to my advantage. Tom Gillispie, A. J. Paul, and I set up on a power line cut near Seward to do some bear calling. In the spring, bears often respond to the sound of a wounded snowshoe hare. We could see up the power line at least seventy-five yards. That was the upwind direction. Downwind we could only see fifteen yards. The crosswind directions weren't much better. We could see maybe thirty yards.

After thirty minutes of calling, we began to hear twigs snapping. The bear came in from the left, circling downwind, moved to our right, and then slowly moved off. We never saw it though it was within thirty yards of us for at least five minutes. In this case, paying attention to wind direction was not sufficient. We needed to pick a location where we had better visibility. This particular bear was a brown bear that left tracks at least nine inches wide. We were probably lucky that the bear was not really hungry. A very large, very hungry bear at very close range might have created a very uncomfortable situation.

Another reason to pay attention to wind direction is so that you can properly set up camp. Terrain and vegetation can be used to your advantage to help protect camp from strong winds. If you are flying into a hunting location, ask the pilot which way the winds tend to blow. Resist the temptation to pitch your tent completely out in the open on a calm day. Tomorrow, it is likely that the wind will be howling.

We succumbed to that temptation on top of Iowa Ridge, just north of the Alaska Range. It was a perfect day when we arrived, sunny with a very light breeze. Tom and Juli Gillispie and I decided to put the tent up high so that we could see a lot of countryside from camp. We had a three-person tent with an external aluminum pole frame. The following morning the wind was blowing so hard that the frame and tent were slapping us in our sleeping bags. The tent was blowing completely flat. Breaking camp in a high wind isn't my idea of fun. But, we had to do it. Moving downslope into a protected swale, we reestablished camp.

On another occasion, Marsha, my son Jason, and I landed at Becharof Dunes on the Alaska Peninsula. This is an area of perpetual wind. We erected the tent in a swale between two sand dunes, out of the worst of the winds. Returning from a morning hunt, Marsha and I found the tent lying almost flat, flapping in the wind with one fiberglass tent pole broken. After repairing the pole with fiberglass strapping tape, we got out a handsaw, sawed our way into an alder thicket, and set up the tent again. This time, it was sufficiently protected.

Of course, wind speed and direction have everything to do with landing sites on fly-in hunts. The landing strip atop Iowa Ridge is nothing more than the bare, gravel summit of a terminal moraine from the ice-age glaciation. The summit runs east to west; the predominant winds come from the south. Takeoffs and landings with light winds are no problem. In a gale, they are virtually impossible.

At the end of one Iowa Ridge hunt, we were waiting for winds to abate so the plane could return for us. There were several parties at the strip. We had flown in with a Helio Courier. Another party arrived in a Super Cub. The Super Cub flew by to check conditions, and we held out strips of surveyor's flagging to indicate wind direction: directly perpendicular to the ridge top. The gravel was perhaps thirty yards wide, and the pilot decided to land into the wind.

He did a great job of slightly exceeding wind speed on his approach. The plane was almost hovering as it hit the gravel. He kept the engine revving while Dale Guthrie, A.J., and I held onto the wing struts and the tail. The hunter quickly got in with his gear. The pilot revved the engine higher with the brakes on. Finally, he gave us the signal to let go. As we jumped aside, the plane took three bounces and was airborne. We paced the take-off distance at about fifty-five feet!

Finally, wind speed and wind gusting can be dangerous because the winds can actually blow you over. I was hiking up Mt. Healy on the ridge above Bison Gulch with a lightly loaded, external-frame pack. The winds were variable, and as I rounded a corner, just about to reach a low saddle on the ridge, a sudden gust of wind caught the pack and lifted me completely off the ground. I landed ten feet away on a talus slope. Thank heavens I wasn't up on a pinnacle at that moment!

I will tell one last wind story. Marsha, Jason, and I were packing a caribou up a steep ridge toward our camp that was on the other side. A strong wind was blowing in our faces as we climbed. When I reached the crest, the wind blew me over. I dropped my pack and turned back to help Marsha and Jason. They had seen me go down and had decided to crawl instead of attempting to walk. We crawled for fifty yards until we could get out of the worst of the gusts.

Be aware:

Which way (and how hard) is the wind blowing?

6

Don't Run a Half Marathon the Day before the Hunt

In high school, I ran track, focusing primarily on hurdles and sprint relays. These are not the best events to build the stamina needed for sheep hunting or for packing moose. However, in college, the hurdling saved my bacon. One night, I hurdled a four-foot hedge to get away from a nasty drunk with a meat cleaver. The incident unfolded outside a bar called The Beer Cave, but that is another story.

I also jogged sporadically through my twenties and thirties. In my midforties, I joined a really great exercise club in Fairbanks, Fit City. The first session was taught by a bouncy, vivacious, young woman who had actually been a student in one of my classes at the university. She was so enthusiastic that I got excited and did every move she did with about the same enthusiasm as she exhibited. At the first heart-rate check, my pulse was 220 per minute. She could tell by the look on my face that I had overshot my target heart rate significantly. The point is this: aerobic exercise programs are not sissy, wimpy, or easy. They can be as demanding as your body can tolerate. Virtually all of these programs can be modified for either high- or low-impact. Shortly after, I started running organized races and found that the breathing rhythms I developed from running worked well when packing. Therefore, hunters, get started if you have not already.

My point is this: running can come in pretty handy for a hunter. One opening day, Russ Shoemaker, Dale Guthrie, and I had spotted two bull caribou a mile or more away and had been hiking steadily toward them. We had to dip down into a saddle and climb a moderately steep ridge to get above the animals. Dale and I were in pretty good shape. Russ wasn't. As we neared the top of the final ridge, the two caribou suddenly appeared about fifteen yards to our left. Apparently, the wind had shifted, carrying our scent around the dome, and they had come to investigate.

Russ, the designated shooter, was pretty excited. It would be his first caribou. He was also pretty winded. The caribou was standing head-on. At the shot, the bigger bull shook his head violently, turned and ran. Both caribou disappeared in seconds. We sprinted around the dome to catch up with them. After about three hundred yards, we came in sight of the two, ambling at a moderate pace.

I threw down my pack, rested my rifle across it, and told Russ to lie down and shoot. But Russ was not there. Dale and I had run off and left him. Several minutes later, he showed up, lay down, and shot one of the bulls.

"I didn't know you had to be a track star to hunt caribou," he said.

Dale and I were nonplussed. It had not occurred to either of us that any hunter might show up on the opening day of caribou season out of shape. Cardio-vascular fitness improves your hiking, packing, and shooting.

Incidentally, the big bull shook his head because Russ's bullet went through the fleshy part of its left ear, obviously not a killing shot. His aim had wobbled off-target by about five inches at fifteen yards because he was breathing hard and shooting offhand. By the next hunt, Russ was in better shape.

A few years after the incident with Russ and Dale, I had another opportunity to employ sprinting to catch up to game. Dale and I had stalked two Dall sheep rams. Both were bedded down, but they were

separated by about one hundred yards. Dale had the first shot and wanted the broomed, old ram about eighty yards upslope from us. My ram was also about one hundred yards away, just below a low ridge. I couldn't see it. Dale shot and said his ram was down. I started running toward my ram's location assuming that he would be up and running away. Just ahead was a shallow ravine I needed to negotiate. Dale's sheep, rolling down the ravine, and I, sprinting to the gully, arrived at the same moment. I hurdled the ravine and sheep and kept on going. By the time I saw the ram, I was within twenty-five yards. All I could see in the scope was white hair. After moving the scope around to find the chest, I shot, and the sheep went down.

One of the problems with hunting and running in interior Alaska is that some of the more interesting runs are scheduled near or during hunting season. How into running are you? Are you willing to miss the last day of moose season to do the Equinox Marathon? The Santa Claus Half Marathon in North Pole has, in the past, been held on the Saturday near or on opening day of sheep and caribou seasons. In hunting, as in real life, there are always choices to be made.

One year back in the 1990s, the Santa Claus Half Marathon was run on August 9, the day before caribou season opened. My friend Paul Matheus and I had our gear packed to drive up the Steese Highway for opening day. He thought I was silly to sign up for the half marathon. He just did not know what a wonderful event it is. The course is flat and well supported by the race organizers. There is even a free barbeque at the end.

I ran the race, ate lunch, drove home, loaded hunting gear, and drove over to pick up Paul. The ride up the Steese Highway to the tundra was a little uncomfortable for my stiff legs. We camped out in a willow thicket that offered some protection from the wind and got a little sleep. Next morning, we started hiking and glassing. I could definitely feel the effects of the race: sore quads, sore glutes, sore back. Of course, we spotted several caribou about five miles off the road on a high ridge. As the morning wore on, the caribou disappeared and reappeared. We headed toward them, continually looking for other caribou that might be closer to the road. No such luck.

By 2:00 PM, we were out where the caribou had been when we had first seen them. They were a mile further out. We decided that we (I) had gone far enough. As we ate lunch, the caribou reversed course and came back toward us. Eventually, they ran by us about thirty yards away. Paul got one with his lever-action Marlin 30-30 with open sights. One shot. I passed on the other caribou, figuring that a five-mile return with half a caribou on my back would be plenty enough packing for me. By late afternoon, we were back at the truck.

Indeed, it was more than enough packing. I was sore when the hunt began, and before it was over, I was sorer than that. But wait. There is more! Runners know this interesting fact: the day after the race is bad, but the day after that is worse. Therefore, my Monday after the Saturday race and Sunday hunt was less than wonderful. It was so much less than wonderful that the title for this chapter instantly came to mind when I started writing this book. I'll restate it in case you forgot:

Don't run a half marathon the day before the hunt.

There is another connection for me between the Santa Claus Half Marathon and hunting. The racecourse winds across the Chena Flood Control Project area east of North Pole. Often on race day, the local retriever club is conducting field trials nearby. I ran the race the first year the two events coincided. I was about a mile and a half into the

race, struggling to get my breathing under control and my circulation pumping along. This is the worst part of the race for me. I slowly eased up to a fellow runner, and we ran stride-for-stride for a while. We were both puffing, neither of us talking much. Suddenly a gunshot went off in the distance, obviously part of the field trials.

Trying to make light of our mutual distress, I commented, "Well, they just had to put one of us down."

He deadpanned, "Yeah. Too bad it wasn't me."

How about biking? Biking can be as aerobic as you want to make it. You can eliminate the jarring impact of running by biking unless, of course, your form of biking involves taking a mountain bike through rocky terrain with jumps. I don't need any more bone-jarring impacts. Running and packing, over the years, have taken their toll on my back.

When I retired, we got a golden retriever, and I thought it would be great to bike with him. We would both get quality exercise at the same time. When he was young and not completely trained to heel, I went out biking with him on a leash along Chena Pump Road in Fairbanks. Murphy was doing great but tired near the end of a six-miler. He dropped behind the bike and decided to cross from my right to my left. That is the moment when his leash went into the back wheel. Of course, the bike stopped instantly, and I landed on the handlebars. I was a little dazed from bouncing my helmet off the asphalt, and I quickly realized that my ribs weren't feeling very good. Several were cracked.

Just like running a long race, the day after you crack ribs is less than wonderful. The second day is even less wonderful than the first day. Unfortunately, the second day after the bike accident was September 1, opening day of moose season. Marsha and I were to hunt with our friends Paul and Toos in a low valley (insert the word "swamp") on opening morning. How bad could it be? Walk around in the swamp for a while, get tired, go home. Not this time.

By 6:30 AM, Paul had a bull down in about a foot of water. The good news, and the bad news, is that the bull went down on a little finger of high ground. The butchering went OK, but then we started to pack loads out through water deep enough to go over our boot tops. The first 150 yards was close to dreadful. Fortunately, it was a young bull. And, fortunately, we had a little less than a mile to pack. With four of us packing, we were finished by 10:30 AM, but my ribs were feeling far less than wonderful! My conclusion:

Biking can get you in shape, but be careful.
And always wear a helmet.

I have one last example of running while hunting. Incredibly, this example does not involve running from bears! Instead, it is about the last day of moose season. I drove out to a dome near Fairbanks for the last afternoon and evening of the moose season. I was sitting on top of the ridge, above tree line, glassing the slopes. A cow and bull moose came out of the willows, heading for the top of the ridge. I estimated that they would cross the ridge about three hundred yards away and that they would not be out of the willows very long. I might have an opportunity to get the bull if I hurried along the ridgeline. Running was the only way to get there. I had a daypack on my back and a rifle. I held the rifle up in front of me, very much like at high port in a military drill, and started running. I'd seen movies involving boot camp, and this seemed pretty similar. As I ran, I quietly sang the cadence: "Am I goin' to shoot a moose? Yes, I'm goin' to shoot a moose! Sound off! One, two! Sound off! Three, four!" The two moose and I arrived at approximately the same point on the ridge at the same time. It was

the biggest bull I ever got. Best of all, I wasn't even winded. Running can be good for your fitness. Just be careful.

Later, I found out that a friend of mine, Pete Terzi, watched the whole jogging episode from a ridge over a mile away. He told me that a far larger bull was not very far downslope from the bull I shot. That is hunting. And, a bull in the pickup is better than a larger bull out in the woods.

As luck would have it, I could get my pickup right up to the bull. Not so luckily, I was by myself. Holding a hind leg up while gutting a moose is backbreaking work. I was straining mightily when a Subaru station wagon pulled up with two berry pickers on board. One of the ladies rolled down the window and asked if I minded them having a close-up look at the moose.

"Not at all. Come on down," I replied. They were fascinated. "Would you ladies be willing to hold up this back leg while I pull the guts out?"

The driver exclaimed, "Oh goody! We'll get to see the guts."

After all the entrails were out, I gave them an anatomical tour of the gut pile. We thanked each other, and they drove off to pick blueberries. When they returned, they stopped and asked if they could call someone for me. I gave them our home phone number and said, "Tell Marsha I'll be late."

7

Sometimes You Can't Go Back to Camp

Short of getting lost, the only situation in which you could not get back to camp by late evening would be, most likely, sheep hunting. I got myself into one of these situations hunting Dall sheep in the Tanana Uplands. The problem, simply stated, is that sheep hunters sometimes walk so far trying to reach a ram that it is pointless or impossible to return to camp by nightfall.

I will describe my circumstance, but first I want to mention one of the other lessons I learned while sheep hunting. The lesson is:

Give bears a wide berth.

Typically, the last thing a sheep hunter wants to do is to tangle with and, God forbid, shoot a bear. Assume for a moment that you are on a sheep hunt and shoot a grizzly, either in defense of life and property or for the trophy. Either way, by law, you must salvage the hide and skull. You will have just added fifty to eighty pounds to your backpack, pushing it to at least one hundred pounds. Adding sheep meat, skull, and cape to such a load is way beyond reason. For most hunters, it would be impossible. Shoot a bear and your sheep hunt is over. *Give bears a wide berth.*

Let me describe the country in which we were hunting. The Tanana Uplands are the hills and mountains between the Tanana and Yukon

Rivers. Mt. Harper is the highest point in the uplands at 6,543 feet elevation. It is the only peak in the Tanana Uplands that had well-developed glaciation during the last ice age.

When I hunted Mt. Harper back in the late seventies and early eighties, the nearest landing strip was a windblown tundra ridge eight miles south of the mountain. There were two routes from the strip to the mountain. For one, you could stay on the tundra and hike around a semi-circle of ridges that added about three miles to the trip. The other, more direct approach required walking off the ridge, bushwhacking to a stream valley, walking eight miles, fording the stream, and climbing back to the tundra. In two successive years, we tried first the circuitous route and then the more direct route.

The second year, the Super Cub dropped Dale Guthrie and me early in the morning. By midday, we were paralleling the stream, enjoying a quiet, sunny day. Before we had an inkling of anything unusual, an F-4 Phantom from Eielson Air Force Base came screaming over our heads. The pilot was flying at treetop level with afterburners! After we buried our shorts, we continued upstream and eventually made camp in a valley on the south flank of the mountain.

We thoroughly glassed the surroundings that evening. There were no sheep, but we did spot a large, blond grizzly a half-mile away. We hoped the bear would drift out of the valley. The next morning, we saw nothing and decided to hike up the mountain. By 2:00 PM, we were high on the mountain glassing far to the north. Two white specks turned out to be legal rams. There was no way to get to them. They were perhaps three miles away.

We started back down toward camp after deciding that we would have to spend the next day moving camp higher up the mountain, closer to the sheep. Our pattern while hiking was for me to lead, Dale to follow. Dale always had an interesting story in progress and, if he

were in the lead, I could not always hear it. Hence, I led. Occasionally, I would interrupt with a shout, "Get out of here, bear!" to make it very clear that there were humans in the vicinity. I did not want to surprise a bear. We were nearing camp as it was nearing twilight. My final "Get out of here, bear!" was pronounced with our light green tent in sight.

"Ron, you don't have to—"

Dale's admonition ended when a large grizzly strolled past our tent and moved off into the brush. *Give bears a wide berth*. If we wanted to sleep in our own tent, we did not have any choice but to continue to approach the tent and the bear. Apparently, we were sufficiently diligent in our handling of food to have prevented the bear from entering the tent or from coming back.

The next morning, we broke camp, packed up, and hiked up onto the west slope of Mt. Harper. We could see the sheep we had seen the previous day, but by the time we had the tent set up and gear organized, it was early afternoon, too late to get to them. We rested in camp and did a lot of glassing that afternoon, hoping to find some closer rams. At 8:30 AM the next morning, we started hiking again. We stayed high on the ridge system heading north toward the sheep. At one point, we crossed a field of boulders. The field was steep, almost at the angle of repose. Several times, as we hopped from one boulder to the next, a boulder would tilt or move downslope several feet. These rocks were large, with diameters of one to four feet. But, by being nimble afoot, we avoided a disabling or potentially lethal mishap.

Hiking steadily with no breaks, we reached the two rams at 4:30 PM. We crept downslope and set up to shoot from about 250 yards. At the first shot, my ram went down, but he managed to struggle to his feet in spite of a lung shot. The second shot put him down for good. Dale decided to take the second ram. One shot was all it took.

By 6:00 PM, the two rams were caped and completely

boned out. The packs were loaded, and we were ready to head back toward camp. At that point, we were at least nine hours from camp. We discussed and immediately rejected the notion of leaving the animals and returning for them the next day.

Sometimes you can't go back to camp.

The overall distance to camp was one problem. The route was another. Neither of us relished tackling the boulder field exhausted and weighted down with sheep meat. Instead, we opted to descend to the valley bottom and ascend the long, winding gulley leading directly back to camp. Losing altitude with a heavy load is a hateful thing to a sheep hunter, but it was our best choice.

We knew we would be out all night so we resolved to hike until it got too dark to see where to put our feet. By 1:15 AM, the long, early autumn twilight finally turned into darkness. We dumped our packs, got out our raincoats, and huddled against a rock until first light at 2:15 AM. The alpenglow at high latitudes really works to the advantage of Alaskan sheep hunters … if you consider the possibility of nearly round-the-clock hiking an advantage.

The climb back to camp was steep, but the footing was, mostly, good. We snacked often to keep our energy levels up. Later that morning, at 10:30 AM, we stumbled into camp. It had been twenty-six hours of almost continuous hiking. During the uphill part, we were carrying a sheep each!

We had hunted out beyond where we expected to be hunting. The extra distance had cost us two days. An additional cost was the twenty-six-hour hike we had just incurred. However, our problems were not over. When we reached camp with the sheep, we had less than twenty-four hours in which to meet our plane … eight miles away.

Some sleep was a must. We decided we could fit an hour and a half rest into our physically challenging day. By 1:00 PM, we were packing camp gear and sheep; the packs weighed about 110 pounds each. Half an hour later, we headed down-valley. We paralleled a boulder-strewn creek that was flanked on each side by lateral moraines, deposited by a late Pleistocene glacier. The tops of the moraines were smooth and relatively free of brush, great for hiking.

A mile down the trail, we stopped for a rest. The shoulder straps really cut on a 110-pound pack. A snack, some water, and a fifteen-minute break, and we would be ready to move on. Right after I shed that heavy pack, I felt almost weightless, heady, exhilarated. The exhilaration vanished in an instant as I watched a huge grizzly drift out of the brush below us. It was a half-mile down the moraine feeding slowly and deliberately on blueberries. Eventually he disappeared from view to the left of the trail. This was easily the largest bear I have ever seen in interior Alaska. The last thing we needed was a close encounter with a large bear while carrying large piles of bloody meat!

Dale and I helped each other up with our heavily laden packs. As I adjusted my waist belt, I was thinking: *give bears a wide berth*. The thought was so prominent that it was verging on that inner scream I mentioned in an earlier chapter. Since I was the leader, I automatically abandoned the moraine we had been following, the left one, and started across the creek toward the other moraine.

"Where are we going, Ron?"

"Across to the other moraine," I answered.

"Why?"

"To get away from that bear," I answered.

"He's not a problem. He's long gone."

"Maybe, but as long as I'm in the lead I'm going down the right moraine," I replied.

In another hour, we had intersected a larger creek, turned left, and found a resting spot. We sat down at the very bottom of the left moraine we had originally been following. Out of curiosity, I started glassing that trail.

"Dale, look up the moraine about five hundred yards, right on the trail, under those three spruce trees."

"What do you see?"

"The grizzly, Dale We would have stepped on him!"

Give bears a wide berth.

The rest of the afternoon and early evening passed as we toiled down the stream. By 10:00 PM, we began the two-mile climb to the airstrip. We angled ever uphill in more or less a straight line toward our destination. With a mile to go, we intersected a ravine we needed to traverse. As we started across, a grizzly exploded from the alders just ahead of us. It followed the exact line we needed to pursue to reach the strip. With no stomach for any more bear encounters, we decided to head straight uphill. Three steps and stop for a breather. Another three steps and stop for a breather. We were very tired by this point.

Nearing twilight, we had topped the ridge and traversed the final mile of tundra to our pickup point. As I recall it, we decided to sleep under the stars rather than unpack the tent. We were beyond tired. We were played out. In the final twenty-four hours, we had covered about fourteen miles of rugged landscape, most of it with 110-pound packs. We had learned (or had had reinforced) two lessons: *give bears a wide berth* and *sometimes you can't get back to camp.*

I have a few, final thoughts about circumstances that could prevent you from getting back to camp. Blizzards with their associated white-outs

may make it difficult or impossible to return to camp, although a good GPS unit could help. Another bad combination for hunters is darkness accompanied by dangerous terrain, such as cliffs. In Chapter 9, I recount a story involving a blizzard, white-outs, dangerous cliffs, and darkness, all rolled into one. Stay tuned.

Clearly, you need to be prepared by carrying the absolute minimum of survival gear: raincoat and/or jacket, hat, food, gloves and/or mittens, and matches or lighter. I mention matches because building a small fire can be very useful, especially in cold weather. On this particular hunt, matches were useless during our overnight huddle. There was nothing to burn for warmth within five miles of us. And, firewood would have been five miles in the wrong direction!

Nevertheless, a great deal of thought must be expended considering what equipment is absolutely necessary for a sheep hunt or for any fly-in hunt. When the plane leaves, you will survive (or die) on the supplies and equipment you brought (or did not bring). If you plan to hike, you had better be prepared to carry what you need.

8

Keep Track of Your Knife

I went to a science convention in Boston in November of 1993 where I stayed in a fancy hotel in Copley Place and did not go outdoors for three days. The hotels and shopping malls were all hooked together by indoor walkways. I felt like a fish out of water! Passing through a mall one afternoon, I spied a cutlery shop and stopped in to look at the hunting knives. There was an odd assortment of kitchen knives, toenail clippers, and such.

I was looking at a few custom-made sheath knives when I overheard a lady say to the proprietor, "Well you don't have nail files, but you have THOSE!" pointing to the custom knives. "What would anyone DO with a knife like that, anyway?"

I instantly answered, "Ma'am, you could gut, skin, and bone out an entire moose with one of these!" Her look of shock turned to disgust, and she fled without another word. I turned back to the knife case, and the proprietor was glaring at me.

He said, "Sir, these are *art knives*."

My response was, "Who the heck is Art?"

I own a lot of knives, but by no stretch of the imagination, am I a knife collector. Especially, I am not a collector of art knives. I am just too practical to own a knife that I put in a box and wipe off occasionally. Hunters and fisherpersons may have some specific requirements for their cutlery that depend on what they intend to do with them and how much weight they expect to be carrying. There is a variety of knives, including pocketknives, Swiss Army knives, sheath knives, and survival knives. Of these different varieties, I think that large sheath knives and survival knives are the most overrated and pocketknives are the most underrated.

First, if weight is a significant consideration, pocketknives can provide great value in terms of utility. Sheep hunters spend a lot of time agonizing over the weight of every single item they put into their backpacks or expect to carry on their persons. Each extra pound will take its toll on a week to ten-day backpacking sheep hunt. A folding knife with one or two blades is easily carried in your pants pocket or a side pocket on your backpack. It has the flexibility to slice cheese and sausage for lunch, process your sheep or caribou, and even do some brush clearing if you need to.

On one sheep hunt in interior Alaska, my partner and I crept up on two decent rams at about six in the evening. We got both rams from the same perch up in the rocks. As we picked our way down the boulder and scree-littered slope, we decided to tackle the processing of each sheep as a team. We pulled out our pocketknives and began to cape and skin. With the hide off, we boned the meat off the carcass and, after that, disconnected the head from the neck. A little bit of whittling on the head to remove as much weight as we could and we were ready to move on to the other ram. All told, we took just over two hours to get those sheep caped, skinned, boned, and in the packs ready to go. Maybe we could have done a little better or faster job with sheath knives. I do not know. I would rather carry a pocketknife with a backup pocketknife than a sheath knife of the same approximate total weight on an extended backpacking hunt. You just have more blades for the weight.

My first knife was given to me at Christmas 1951. My brother Rob and I got identical, "genuine" Bowie knives with six-inch blades and black bakelite handles. The bakelite was jigged to make it look like bone, but it did not look like bone. It looked like black plastic. But, we were both thrilled. I am amazed that I still have that knife, especially considering how many other knives have passed through my hands since then.

My first recollection of using that knife for its intended purpose was in August of 1957. Before that August, we had thrown the knives at tree trunks, whittled, and played mumbley-peg. Now, at fourteen years old, I was going on my first real deer hunt where I could use the knife like an adult. Rob and I got in his 1950 DeSoto and headed for the San Gabriel Mountains at 4:00 AM.

It was pitch black, but the sky was filled with meteors falling to earth. We were looking at the height of the Perseid Meteor Shower, an annual August event that peaks every eleven years, and 1957 was a peak year. I told my brother it was a good omen. He laughed.

He pulled the car off a dirt road in a canyon, and we assembled our gear: rifle, candy bar, canteen, and Bowie. I figured out later that he didn't really want to hunt with me. He explained that our chances would be better if we split up.

"Which way do you want to go? he asked.

"I'll go uphill into those ponderosa pines," I said.

He said, "OK, I'll go the other way."

It was very dark, but I climbed up to a knoll and sat down, buttoning up my jacket. August in the California desert is hot during the day and pretty chilly at night. Just after dawn, I heard something coming down the steep slope behind me. A mule deer buck ran down the slope and up the knoll upon which I sat. As he passed broadside, I shot. The deer went down nearby, and I gutted it with my "genuine" Bowie.

Not knowing what to do next, I grabbed my rifle, hiked down to the car, and left a note for my brother, telling him I was dragging a deer down to the road. Back I went up the hill. But halfway up, I spotted another buck standing off the trail. Since it was a two-buck area, I shot it too.

Obviously, the next move was to gut the second deer. I put my hand on the sheath, but the knife wasn't there. I had left it with the first deer.

Keep track of your knife.
Keep it with you at all times.

Now what? Fortunately, I heard a vehicle on the road just below me. I ran down to the road and flagged down the jeep. Four adult hunters piled out and asked if I needed help. I asked to borrow a knife so I could field dress my deer.

"Sure, son. Let's have a look at your deer. We haven't seen a thing."

Instead of just lending me a knife, several of the men did the work for me. I must have looked as if I needed help. As they finished dragging the gut pile away from the deer, one of the men asked how I managed not to have a knife with me.

"I'm sorry for your trouble. I left it with the first deer I shot this morning."

Not another word came out of any of the four men. They got in their jeep and drove away. If I had remembered my knife, I could have spared those guys their frustration. *Keep track of your knife.*

Decades later, Dale Guthrie and I were standing on a limestone pinnacle jutting out toward the Yukon River, looking for a ram that had given us the slip. We climbed down and moved downslope until we were nearly into the spruce. I saw a movement down in the trees to my left. It was the ram. After Dale's successful shot, we got out the game bags and knives and went to work. I used my favorite, wood-handled pocketknife. As we finished, it was getting dark, the wind was howling, and it started to rain. We packed up in a hurry; camp was a mile above us. I walked away and left that knife sticking in a clump of bright red bearberry. A storm blew in, and I never recovered my knife. *Keep track of your knife.*

If you get a big game animal down and two people start skinning, be careful! I have been cut by two different guys while trying to mind my own business elsewhere on the carcass. Since few Alaskan hunters have the luxury of hoisting an animal on a gambrel, we end up whittling on a beast that is lying on the ground. If you are skinning on the hind end, send your friend to the front end. In this case, you are keeping track of the other guy's knife. This is so common-sense I'm embarrassed to mention it.

I mentioned gutting and skinning a moose earlier in this chapter. That task is ever so much easier if you have a hunting partner to hold up a hind leg while you remove entrails, skin the inside of the leg, or start to detach the ham from the rest of the carcass. If you don't have a hunting partner but are close to a road, you may be able to get help from someone as I did with the berry-picking ladies I mentioned in an earlier chapter who helped me with a big bull moose.

The initial gutting and/or skinning is made easier with some sort of gut-hook blade. The hook is inserted into a starter hole on the abdomen or hind leg. A steady pull on the knife results in the "unzipping" of the hide. You try to cut as few hairs as possible when processing a game animal. You can accomplish the same task without a gut-hook by inserting the point of an ordinary blade into the starter hole with the sharp edge of the blade pointing away from the animal. In any case, you need to keep track of the knifepoint. Otherwise, you might puncture the abdominal organs and get a nasty face full of foul gas and/or liquid. *Keep track of your knife.*

I mentioned being cut by several friends while skinning, but I am embarrassed to admit that the worst cut I ever got butchering was self-inflicted. My son Jason had shot a caribou an hour before the plane was due to pick us up. After we skinned and gutted the animal, I sent him back to camp to pack gear and haul a load to the airstrip. I was cutting meat off the bones, working too rapidly … carelessly. The blade sliced across my thumb instead of caribou meat. I had never seen any of my own bones before that moment. There was a lot of blood everywhere; only some of it belonged to the caribou. *Keep track of your knife*!

The easiest way to lose your knife is to lay it down next to a big gut pile or next to parts of a carcass that are being moved around. If the gut pile ends up on top of your knife, you may never see it again.

This leads me to mention knife handles. Specifically, what is the handle made of and what color is it? If the handle material is smooth, such as is the case with phenolics or polished wood, it may be very slippery when covered with blood. There are several handle materials that provide a good grip even when wet. These rubber or Kraton handles work well but, perhaps, are not the most attractive.

The color of the handle material is also important. For the life of me, I cannot understand why anyone would want a knife with a camouflaged handle. If it is camo, it cannot easily be seen. That is a negative, not a positive.

Several years ago, my wife Marsha gave me what will probably be my last and best hunting knife. The blade is specially serrated and guaranteed never to get dull. If it does get dull, we can mail it back to the manufacturer, and it will be resharpened by hand for free. The handle is a non-slip material that feels like rubber. It works even when wet. It is day-glo orange. I will always be able to *keep track of my knife*!

9

Take Enough Food

When I first started hunting with Dale Guthrie, I (and he) didn't realize that he had a condition called hypoglycemia. Hypoglycemia is a pancreatic hormone malfunction, almost the opposite of diabetes. Dale's body was too efficient at removing sugar from the bloodstream. Eating refined sugar is not good. It is too quickly removed from the circulation. A steady, slow trickle of complex carbohydrates and proteins into the gastrointestinal tract keeps him running well in the field.

On a multi-day hunt, he felt good and performed well by munching more or less continuously.

"Want a handful of peanuts, Ron?"

"No, I'm not hungry right now," I'd reply.

It turned out that halfway through the hunt, with Dale constantly munching, we were almost out of food. Thus my strategy of "defensive eating" was born. *Take enough food.* From then on, I carried plenty of food, and I ate every time Dale did. Then, it became a subtle, unspoken contest to lighten our packs.

"I have these great sandwiches, Dale!"

"OK, I'll have one."

We both ate but, as the food supply diminished, one of us hiked on with a lighter pack. If there were a third person, both Dale and I unloaded as long as we were certain we had enough food. Actually, continual snacking is a really good idea for all active hunters. At any moment, a hiking hunter may be called upon to move vigorously over a considerable distance to intercept some hapless beast. You need to be fueled up for that possibility.

I remember a circumstance in which I should have been snacking more. It involved skinning and butchering a moose on a dome north of Fairbanks. John Fox and I got a moose early in the day and, without stopping, boned the whole thing. Then, with no food intake, we started packing. Pretty soon, we were both exhausted. After a quick sandwich and candy bar, we were rejuvenated.

By far, my most memorable food-related hunt was my one and only winter goat hunt. Ken Whitten, Dale, and I took a week of Christmas break, drove to McCarthy, Alaska, and hunted mountain goats. It was a relatively mild, late December in 1974.

After packing up our gear, including a three-person tent, we headed up the trail to Kennicott, a few miles away. The trail was well packed, and we did not need the snowshoes for this part. We arrived at the camp and met the caretaker for the mine buildings. When he heard we were going to camp out, he generously offered to let us sleep in an empty room in the main building. Since part of the building was heated, we slept inside at +30°F instead of outside at -20°F.

Next day, we struck out onto the Kennicott Glacier. The caretaker had seen goats across the glacier on a pyramid-shaped peak. With a foot of new snow on the ice, we could not accurately locate all the cracks and crevasses. Roped up, we snowshoed over a mile toward the peak. The weather seemed surprisingly benign for -20°. After thoroughly glassing the peak, we could find no goats, no tracks, nothing.

Turning back, we realized we had been moving downwind the whole morning. Facing the wind was far from benign. We cooled down immediately and started eating. Human physiologists have demonstrated that the metabolic rate of a human jumps about 10 percent after eating a meal. Part of that extra metabolism goes into digesting the food, and part goes into heat production. Therefore, if you are hunting in cold weather, *take enough food*.

Three days of tromping around in the snow and eating lots of food resulted in no goats. We did not see a single one. December 30 dawned, and we started the long drive back to Fairbanks. We got to Chitina at sundown, that is, about 3:00 PM. Dale suggested we stop and talk to the pilot at Chitina Air Service. It looked like a warm office so Ken and I agreed.

As luck would have it, the pilot had just flown over the Chugach Mountains from Cordova. He had seen a bunch of goats near a lake he could land on. The lake had a trapper's cabin on one end and goats on the other. It was too late to fly that day, but he could drop us on the lake the next morning. The weather forecast was for a continuation of the same mild, calm conditions we had been experiencing. The pilot offered us his hanger for camping. Unfortunately, it did not have a door, and the temperature dropped to -35° during the night.

Next morning, the pilot ferried us up to the lake. The goats were lounging near the top of a four-hundred-foot cliff just off one end of the lake. The old trapper's cabin was in a tiny grove of spruce trees at the other end. All we had to do was hang out in the cabin until the next morning, snowshoe down to the lake, and collect the goats. The pilot was to return the next evening. That evening, we ate three of our six remaining sandwiches. I insisted we save the two pounds of raisins until after we got the goats. Sometime during the night, the wind started howling.

We woke up to blizzard conditions. Visibility varied from poor to complete white-out. Rather than stay in the cabin, we decided to go down to the lake and look for the goats. It seemed like a good idea at the time. Ken was breaking trail when, suddenly, he simply disappeared. I was astonished. I was right behind him. Where could he have gone? I took one more step, and from Dale's perspective as last in line, I also vanished. Dale recalls thinking, "Wow! I wonder where those guys went!" Ken and I had walked off the edge of a twenty-foot cliff. Luckily, we both escaped unhurt. The snowdrifts had cushioned our fall, and I had narrowly missed landing on Ken. A second lesson of this chapter might be:

Don't snowshoe in a white-out.

We regrouped. Clearly, if we could walk over a twenty-foot cliff in a white-out, we could just as easily walk off the four-hundred-foot cliff somewhere ahead.

Ken summed it up: "Forget the goats. Let's go back to the cabin!"

I led up a moderately steep slope. Halfway up, I remarked, "Guys, I can hear water rushing underneath my snowshoes. That's bad, right?"

We moved ever so carefully to the top and continued on until we got to the edge of the lake. After a quick break devoted to eating the last of our now frozen sandwiches, we pressed on, keeping the shore of the lake on our right. Another forty-five minutes traversing the lake brought us to an unexpected and unwelcome sight: partially covered tracks of several sets of snowshoes. The tracks were ours. What to do?

Dale suggested we dig a snow cave and wait out the storm.

I countered, "I'm getting cold while we are snowshoeing. If we stop I'll get colder." We turned our attention to how we had gotten lost in the first place. It finally occurred to us that the lake we saw from the plane wasn't a simple ovoid shape. Instead, we recalled a constriction near the middle. The lake was shaped like an hourglass. We had been careful to keep outcrops along the shore to our right as we progressed. It appeared that we had crossed the pinched, narrow

part of the lake because we had seen an outcrop across the lake. The periodic white-outs hadn't helped.

Again, we headed down to the lake. This time we figured it out. In the gloom of twilight, we spotted the small clump of spruce. By the time we got to the cabin, it was almost pitch black outside. So far, we had almost died four different ways. However, we had successfully avoided falling off a four-hundred-foot cliff, falling into an ice-cold stream in a blizzard, getting totally lost, and developing hypothermia. But, as they say in the television ad, "Wait! There's more!" In our case, the final challenge was the food supply.

We were in the middle of a blizzard with no sign of it letting up. The cabin had a small wood stove but there was no chimney projecting above the roof. We could build a small fire, but every few minutes the fifty-mile-per-hour wind would blow lots of smoke down into the cabin, forcing us to open the cabin door. The cabin never got above 0° although we could melt snow on the stove.

The remaining food consisted of the two one-pound boxes of raisins. One of us suggested that we eat one box and save the other for the next few days. Since I had possession of the raisins, I insisted that I dole them out pretty conservatively. We finally arrived at three meals a day, ten raisins each per meal. None of us was happy with that ration, but we had no idea how long we might be stuck in that cabin.

The snow fizzled out on our third day in the cabin. The wind continued to howl, and the temperature dropped to -50°. Over the next six days we spent in that cabin, we had lots of time to talk.

On the first day, we argued about the proper way to eat a ten-raisin meal. We discovered that, in high school, each of us had been on the track team and each had run high hurdles. Dale took the lead in reminiscing over great food he had eaten in the past. Juicy steaks figured prominently in our conversations. I recounted a long-ago date I had with Marilyn, the woman who would become my first wife. The date was a picnic during which we were grilling large T-bone steaks on a barbeque. During a lapse in our attention, Marilyn's old Dalmatian, Spot, snagged one of the steaks and consumed it within fifteen seconds. Both Dale and Ken groaned, thinking about my loss.

On the third day, the conversation turned to cannibalism. Dale brought it up jokingly. However, I was the skinniest of the three by far and, therefore, most likely to starve to death first. It did not strike me as a funny topic under the circumstances. After a lengthy discussion, I extracted a promise from each of them that they would let me die naturally rather than "assisting" the process. A scene from *Monty Python and the Holy Grail* came up repeatedly in conversation. It was the scene in which two men are calling out, "Bring out your dead."

Of course, every time we kicked open the door to get some fresh air, we looked out to see if a caribou, goat, ptarmigan, or anything edible might be lingering around the doorway. One day, we heard a raven calling nearby. That triggered an intense discussion about the possibility of shooting and eating a raven. We were weakening by then and decided it was too risky and energy-demanding to make a try for the raven. *Take enough food.*

With the wind howling, we continually hallucinated about airplanes flying over the cabin. Meanwhile, our pilot was grounded, first by the blowing snow and then by the wind. On the seventh day, the airplane sounds were real. When he landed, we still had a pound of raisins, and I had dropped from 150 pounds to 134, a loss of 17 pounds. I could recommend this experience as the ultimate weight loss challenge, the ultimate fat farm. Instead, I will stick to: *take enough food.*

By the way, the drive back to Fairbanks was nightmarish. In Chitina, the pickup was very frozen. Two hours of a blasting space heater got it warm enough to start. We drove to Gakona Junction and stopped

at the only roadhouse. Ken ordered: "Burgers, fries, and pie for all of us!" Unfortunately, we could barely get through the burgers. The fries and pie went in a "to go" bag. Our stomachs had shrunk quite a bit during the blizzard.

Passing through Delta Junction, we had the option of stopping for gas or hoping we would make it all the way to Fairbanks. Since I had a five-gallon gas can in the back of the truck and nobody wanted to pump gas at -60°, we drove on. That was a mistake. We had just passed the old south gate to Ft. Wainwright when the gas ran out. The temperature had dropped to -65°. I got out and poured the gas into the truck, jumped back in, and tried to start it, but it wouldn't start. The starter motor was frozen. Another bout of hypothermia ensued before we were able to flag down one of the very few trucks still on the road. Final count: we almost died five different ways. *Take enough food.*

That winter goat hunt provided another take-home lesson for me. Before the hunt, I had a deep sense of foreboding. I worried. I sensed that events were not going to unfold well. There was nothing specific I could pinpoint. We had enough gear, extra gasoline and, at least initially, enough food. *Listen to your inner scream*, although "scream" is too strong a word here. I recall hearing a voice. I'm nervous about admitting that, once in a while, I have heard a voice inside my head suggesting a course of action. The voice, on this particular occasion, was emphatically stating that the winter goat hunt was a bad idea. I could soft-peddle the lesson by simply stating: if it sounds like a really bad idea, it is, very probably, a really bad idea.

I am certain that I would have stayed home that December if I had remembered an earlier incident in which I heard an actual voice inside my head. That incident unfolded when I was seventeen years old. It was a dark and stormy night. Really. I had gassed up my 1950 DeSoto and was about to turn left onto a road that would take me home. Through the wipers, I could see a set of headlights in the distance on my left. The car was too far away to pose a problem. I started to ease out on the clutch and press on the accelerator, starting to turn left. Before I could complete the motion, I heard a distinct voice inside my head. It was a Charlton Heston-like voice. I am not making this up. There was only one word: "**Stop!**" I immediately hit the brakes and looked again to my left. A second set of headlights had appeared, coming at incredible speed. The second car was moving in excess of one hundred miles per hour. If I had turned left as I originally intended, I would have been part of a spectacular, head-on collision.

Listen to your inner scream,
especially if it is telling you to
take enough food!

10

Hunt Up to the End

Finally! The winds that had pounded us for four days had, at last, moderated. We had hunted in driving wind and rain the first day and had moved camp to a more protected location on the second. The remaining two days were spent inside the tent. The hunt had been a bust, but at least, the Super Cub would be able to land on the ridge and retrieve us.

The pilot was due to pick us up that very morning. I looked out of the tent flap and saw thin clouds hanging on the ridge tops. Might as well get up and do a little glassing before we broke camp.

Through the thin fog, I could barely see the saddle below us. Two caribou were making their way through the willows and spruce, coming our way. My son Jason was still in the sleeping bag. I whispered for him to get in his rain pants and boots. He came out with his rifle in time for us to move to a clearing with a view. The bull walked by us at a distance of sixty yards. Jason shot, and the bull went down.

I expected to hear the airplane engine at any moment so we went to work. We gutted and skinned that bull in a hurry. Jason went back to the tent and packed gear while I cut meat off the carcass. We met up with our loaded packs just as the plane settled onto the gravel strip.

As the plane took off with Jason, meat, and gear, I returned to the caribou. After finishing the butchering, I packed the remaining meat to the runway and returned to the tent. Then it was simply a matter of waiting until I heard the plane returning for me. At the first drone of the engine, I dropped the tent, packed it and my sleeping bag, and trotted up to the strip.

The point is:

Don't give up. Hunt right up to the end.

I remember two years in which I got bull moose in failing light on the last day of the season. More than a few caribou hunts were successful late in the evening at the last possible moment of shooting light. By the way, leave your tent up until your plane is actually on the ground. If the plane is delayed, you have a place to sit out of the rain and wind.

An example of a hunt on which success came late in the day was a caribou hunt west of Iliamna Lake. Marsha, Jason, Tom Gross, and I had spent the day hunting for a decent bull. After a late dinner, we decided to turn in. Marsha, Jason, and I were in the tent; Tom hadn't quite given up.

Suddenly, Tom cried out, "Jason, grab your rifle! There is a really nice bull on the skyline!" He eased his rifle out the tent opening, crawled out, and shot. It was the biggest bull caribou he has ever gotten. We butchered it with the aid of flashlights. *Don't give up. Hunt right up to the end.*

The first day of October (and the first day of a two-day cow season) found Dale Guthrie, John Fox, and me tracking a cow and calf moose up a snowy ridge in interior Alaska. We were a mile off the road, climbing steadily.

"Time for a snack, guys," Dale remarked. We sat down on our packs and glassed the canyon below while we ate. One of us spotted a cow down in the valley about a mile away.

John wondered aloud, "Should we go after that cow or keep following these other two?" We quickly agreed to pursue the animal we could actually see. Soon, two other moose appeared with the first, another cow and a young bull.

We were halfway to the valley floor when we began to hear an all-terrain-vehicle. It came up the valley bottom and stopped directly opposite the moose. We were crestfallen. One of us suggested that we immediately turn around and pick up the trail we had recently abandoned.

"Hold on. Let's watch this scene play out. Maybe the extra cow will come our way," I suggested. We sat on our packs and watched the other hunter pick up his rifle and walk toward the moose. He stopped about fifty yards from the bull, stood there for a few minutes, then turned and walked back to his machine. We were dumbfounded when he drove away without firing a shot.

Down the ridge we went. At the bottom, we came to an eight-foot wide stream, still unfrozen. John was wearing leather boots and waded across. Dale and I were wearing military canvas mukluks. We took them off first. On the other side we re-donned our mukluks, stomped our feet to try to get some feeling back, and went after the moose.

As we approached, the bull was standing. We saw one cow lying down, and I handed my rifle to John. The cow jumped up, and John shot. It did not go down immediately so he shot again. Both bullets went through the lungs. As the first cow crumpled, the second cow sprang to her feet. John handed the rifle back to me, and I shot. After staggering a few yards, the second cow went down. If we had been discouraged by the hunter on the ATV, we would not have gotten those two moose. *Don't give up.*

Retrieving those two cows was interesting. We gutted and skinned both, and each carried a load of meat back to the road. It was well after dark, so after grabbing a burger at a nearby roadhouse, we decided to come back the next day and finish the packing. Next day, I loaded a few sheets of three-quarter-inch plywood in the truck, picked up John and Dale, and headed back. When we arrived at the canyon, we placed the plywood sheets on the partially frozen soil and drove the truck onto them. As I drove forward, John and Dale kept shifting the plywood ahead so that we could keep the truck on top. Eventually, we arrived at the kill site, loaded all the moose parts, and returned to the road. We did not get stuck, did not dig ruts in the muskeg, and did not have to pack the two moose on our backs.

To celebrate, we pulled into the same roadhouse and, again, bought burgers. The proprietor, having heard our story the previous night, had a question.

"Are you sure those were cows?"

"Yes. Cows don't have antlers. Bulls do," I answered.

"Yeah," he continued. "But the guy you saw on the ATV yesterday stopped in after you left. He swore there were no cow moose up the valley. Only the bull. He turned you guys in to Fish and Wildlife Protection."

I asked him, "Do you have a minute? I want to show you something." He followed me outside. In the light shining through the windows, he could clearly see the two cow moose heads in the back of the pickup. "Any questions?"

"Nope."

We took all the meat to Dale's house to let it hang for a few days. Quarters were hung in his garage alongside a big hog he had just skinned,

beheaded, and gutted. When the officer knocked on Dale's door, he asked if Dale could clear up the complaint. Dale invited him into the garage where the officer gazed fixedly at the skinned, beheaded hog.

"What is that thing?" he finally asked.

"Fish and Wildlife Protection officer," Dale answered with a straight face.

The officer laughed nervously and jumped when Dale slapped him on the shoulder and said, "Just kidding! It's a big hog."

"OK, I can see the cow moose heads. That's enough for my report." He left in a hurry.

Marsha, Jason, and I did our most recent fly-in caribou hunt in 2004. As we had done several times before, we flew a scheduled airline to Iliamna and chartered an air taxi to drop us off on a likely lake. The hunting had not been good that fall, and the last party to hunt this particular lake had stayed a week and gotten skunked.

On the next to the last day, we spotted and eventually intercepted three caribou. We shot, and all three went down within a hundred yards of camp. We carried the meat to a makeshift drying rack, ate dinner, and turned in.

The last day of the hunt, we hunted hard. Three caribou would not get us through the winter. We could really use a few more. For at least twelve hours, we hiked, sat, glassed, and repeated the sequence. The sun was low in the west when we headed to camp. It was nearly dinnertime, and we were tired and hungry.

Just before we reached camp, we spotted five caribou on the other side of our lake. Should we let them go? After a short discussion, we decided to go after them. We were going to *hunt right up to the end.*

It took a mile-and-a-half hike and a hundred-yard crawl to get into position. Jason shot one, and I shot another. We butchered and packed them both to a single location we could find again. The three of us were able to pack one animal back to camp that evening. We would have to come back for the second, but before we got back to camp, the light failed completely. We broke out our flashlights for the last three hundred yards.

Clearly, it was too late to go back for the remaining meat that night. Our plane was due to return for us bright and early the next morning. We resolved to get up at dawn. Marsha would break camp and get it down to the lake. Jason and I would hike out and get the last loads of meat. The outbound hike was made difficult by ground fog, but we had a few good landmarks to guide us. We were halfway back to camp with the meat when George landed the Beaver. Most of our gear was loaded in the plane when Jason and I reached it. Don't give up.

Hunt right up to the end.

11

Who Is Going to Shoot?

The snapping of twigs and movement of brush was no more than twenty feet away. The episode had begun forty-five minutes earlier when A. J. Paul first blew on the predator call. We were standing on the edge of an old logging clear-cut. The second growth was seven feet tall, and we could only see about ten feet into the undergrowth. After ten minutes, A.J. blew the call again, and we started hearing the sounds of an approaching animal.

The twenty feet became fifteen, then ten. The head of a black bear thrust itself out of the undergrowth and looked directly at me. "Why didn't A.J. shoot?" I thought. The bear turned to look at A.J. At that moment, he was wondering why I did not shoot. The bear's head disappeared into the brush, and we spent the next ten minutes listening to the bear sounds moving away.

When we no longer heard the bear, A.J. asked, "Why didn't you shoot?"

I responded, "Why didn't YOU shoot?"

Well in advance of the shooting, decide:

Who is going to shoot.

The opposite end of the spectrum is when both shooters actually shoot. There are circumstances in which a follow-up shot by a second shooter is highly desirable. It is great to discuss these circumstances with your hunting partner ahead of time.

An incident in which the discussion occurred only after the fact happened to me many years ago. A friend who had never slain a bear wanted to go bear hunting. I had bagged four or five bears by then, so I told him that he would be the shooter but I would take my rifle.

We were glassing berry patches above tree line when the black bear appeared. He was over a mile away. We began a long stalk. Halfway there, we could still see the bear. Shortly after that, we lost him. We turned back and immediately saw the bear standing a hundred yards away. Fred (I'll call him Fred, but that's not his real name) raised his rifle and shot. Instantly the bear was running, favoring its left, front leg. It looked as if Fred had hit the lower front leg, not a lethal hit at all.

At the moment the bear started running, I began raising my rifle, reasoning that if the bear reached heavy brush we would never find him. The crosshairs found the bear just as he turned straight away and plunged into the willows. My rifle went off with the cross squarely in the middle of the black mass.

My shot surprised and angered Fred. He had not wanted me shooting his bear. I tried to explain my thinking based on what had just unfolded and suggested we needed to follow up on the wounded bear. We waited five minutes and went into the willows. The bear had traveled thirty yards. It was still alive but was unable to move. Fred finished it with one final shot.

Indeed, Fred's shot had broken the left front paw. My shot had entered the left ham about two inches from dead center on the retreating beast. The bullet went forward and stopped in the left front shoulder near the ribs. It had clipped one lung.

I am convinced that without my follow-up shot we would have lost the bear. Bears are tough animals. Since that hunt, I have always tried to make it clear *who is going to shoot* and, on bear hunts, that there will be a back-up shot if it runs.

Many years after the episode with Fred, on the same mountain, I spotted another bear in a berry patch. I hiked over to it and then crept until I was about seventy-five yards away. I laid my rifle over my pack and watched the bear through the scope for a while. Then I watched through my binoculars. Bears are really interesting creatures to watch. After four or five minutes, the wind shifted, and the bear caught my scent and took off running. Dang! I had forgotten to shoot! If you are hunting, decide *who is going to shoot*, and then, *don't forget to shoot*.

Caribou hunting is often a meat-hunting proposition. In my mind, getting the animal down in a humane fashion is critically important. Bragging rights for the kill are unimportant.

Another incident in which these two approaches to hunting, a humane kill versus bragging rights, unfolded on a caribou hunt. An acquaintance and I were hunting north of Fairbanks in the early fall. We drove up an old mining road and stopped in a saddle to glass for caribou. My hunting partner (a different "Fred" this time) refused to use his binoculars because a) he expected me to do the game spotting and b) there were several parties camping near the saddle. In his mind, if there were any caribou nearby, these other hunters would have seen them.

After several minutes of careful looking, I announced, "A young caribou bull!"

"Where?"

"I won't tell you. You'll have to find it yourself. The only clue I'll give you is that he is south of us."

Five minutes elapsed before he saw it.

Two miles of hiking across the tundra brought us to within two hundred yards of the lone caribou. I'd seen this guy shoot on the way up the road earlier in the day and knew that he needed a rock-solid rest. We took off our packs and stacked them for a shooting rest. He lay down behind them and got control of his breathing … I thought.

At the shot, the caribou exhibited a reaction that indicated a gut shot.

"Shoot again," I suggested. Seven more shots followed without another hit. The poor creature lay down for a while, and I prayed it would bleed out and fall over. No such luck. In a few minutes, the bull got up and started climbing over the ridge.

"I'm going to try a shot," I told him.

"I don't want you shooting my caribou," he answered.

"Well, it's wounded, it's suffering, and it's getting away. I'm going to shoot."

"You might hit it in the hams and ruin the meat," he countered.

"Listen," I said, "it's already gut-shot. How much more damage can I do? Besides, if it gets away, ALL the meat will be lost."

No response.

"OK, I'll try a head shot. It'll either be a miss or a kill."

He laughed, and said, "He's out there maybe 250 to 275 yards. You'll never hit the head!"

"Then, what do we have to lose, besides the caribou?"

Reluctantly, he agreed.

As we had argued, I had settled behind the packs. I waited until the bull stopped to start my squeeze. At the shot, the bull went down. We found a hole just under the antlers. My companion cussed me up and down for shooting HIS caribou.

After we finished the butchering, I propped up the head a hundred yards from our packs and made him lie prone and shoot at the head. He hit it squarely with two successive shots.

"Well, at least you can't blame your poor shooting on the rifle," I remarked. We never hunted together again.

12

Trust Your Sighted Rifle

H unters are continually arguing about what is the single most important thing to take on a hunt. I could argue that common sense is the most critical thing you must have. However, anyone who has read this far might find it hard to believe that I would put much stock in common sense. Physical condition is very important. It would be downright embarrassing to complete a perfect stalk, place the perfect killing shot, and then have a heart attack trying to pack out the beast. Common sense would dictate: get in shape and don't lift more than you can carry.

Almost at the top of the list: it is absolutely critical that you be very familiar with your gun before you go hunting. I am embarrassed to point this out, but a few hunters I have hunted with did not know this, and we can all use a reminder. The rest of the list that follows seems so common-sense that I would not waste space on it except I have known of hunters that made every mistake in the list. Bear with me.

Rather than listing *don'ts*, I'll make a short list of *dos. Do* take your gun out of its original box before you take it hunting. If the rifle has a scope on it or if you mount a scope on it yourself, *do* assume that it needs to be sighted in. For the totally uninitiated, sighting in a rifle means making the bullets go where the rifle is pointing. Believe me, hunters, we owe it to the animals we harvest to make their passing as quick and painless as possible. A sighted-in rifle in the hands of a competent, thoughtful hunter is, in my mind, a critical and necessary combination.

Back to the list. *Do* use the same ammunition on the hunt that you used to sight in the rifle. Different brands and especially different bullet weights do not have the same point of impact. *Do* insure that, after sighting, the rifle does not get dropped, especially onto its scope. *Do* sight in your own rifle yourself. If you would not trust a friend to pack all your hunting essentials for a fly-in hunt, why would you trust him/her to sight in your rifle?

Another topic of endless argument among hunters is how to actually sight in the rifle. My approach follows that of Jack O'Conner, an outdoor writer from the mid-twentieth century who wrote for *Outdoor Life* magazine. He always sighted his scoped rifles to hit point of aim at 25 yards. With rifles similar to the .30-06 with 180-grain bullets, this sighting method translates, approximately, to dead-on at 25 yards, 1.5 inches high at 100 yards, dead-on again at 220-240 yards, and roughly 3 inches low at 300 yards. Therefore, if a big game animal is within 300 yards, you put the cross hairs where you want the bullet to hit and squeeze the trigger. No complex mental calculations are necessary, no need to hold over or under the point where you wanted the bullet to hit. This means that the effective point-blank range is 300 yards.

O'Conner's method for a rifle with an iron sight was to sight it to hit point of aim at 12.5 yards. No need to hold over your intended impact point until the range exceeded 150 yards. Shooting at a living target beyond 150 yards with open sights is, in my thinking, too chancy to risk.

When I first arrived in Alaska, I hunted with an old, lever-action .30-40 Krag with iron sights. I'd fired a lot of 180-grain bullets through that barrel, and I knew where they hit … up to a point. I had no trouble dropping a caribou at eighty yards, but I did not trust myself or the rifle beyond 150 yards.

Fortunately, there was a long box under the Christmas tree that year, a .30-06 that very quickly wore a telescopic sight. I shot it a lot, followed the O'Conner method for sighting it, and was ready to go the next fall. The first opportunity was an early October caribou hunt. Dale Guthrie and I drove up an old mining road until we reached a washout. Donning our packs, we started hiking, eventually climbing out of the forest into the tundra. The remnants of the road disappeared.

As we climbed, we glassed the snow-filled bowl. During a lunch break, we spied a lone caribou on the skyline. It was a cow. Shortly, she headed down into the bowl followed by nineteen additional caribou. All twenty stopped about three hundred yards away and began pawing through the crusted snow for food.

Even though we both had scoped rifles, we sneaked and, finally, crawled until the distance was only 175 yards.

"No more cover. We are close enough, Ron."

"I'll take the bull on the right; you take the one on the left," I said.

I put the cross hairs on the lung area. Surely I'd get some bullet drop at 175 yards, I thought. I'd better be safe and hold for the top of the back. With the horizontal cross hair lying on the top of the back, the rifle went off. The caribou flinched but, obviously, wasn't hit.

"Shoot again, Ron!"

On the second shot, I did not have time to think. I simply put the cross hairs behind the shoulder and squeezed. The caribou went down within a few seconds, a perfect lung shot. As we approached the two dead bulls, I was curious to see what went wrong with my first shot.

Dale remarked, "Your first shot went exactly where you aimed, Ron. See, you clipped the hair on the top of his back."

Trust your sighted rifle.

Incidentally, the pack out with those caribou was one of the worst of my entire life. There was a thin covering of snow on everything, including an occasional rock. Stepping on spongy tundra lightly covered with snow was fine, but stepping on the rocks usually caused our feet to slip out from under us. We took dozens of falls, and our backs and our pack frames took a beating. My external frame pack started with a frame shaped something like a regular capital H but was definitely an italics H when we finished. I had to buy a new frame.

The next fall, Mom and Dad flew up from California to visit the grandchildren and the grandchildren's parents … in that order. Dad had scheduled the visit so that he would be in Alaska for the opening of caribou season. What ensued turned out to be the most humiliating and disturbing hunt of my life.

On opening day, we headed up the Steese Highway. We took one rifle, the scoped .30-06. When we got to the high country, there were small bands of caribou scattered across the landscape. I maneuvered the Bronco off the mining road and parked. I handed Dad the rifle and loaded my backpack. Finally, we were ready and started hiking after a small band that had just gone over a ridge in the distance. After a mile, we caught up to them. I set Dad up with a prone rest over the pack: rock solid.

What followed was a hunter's worst nightmare. Dad's first shot hit the young bull too far back, a gut shot. He did not go far, but he did not go down either. Additional shots were all misses. We were both frustrated and very unhappy. The bull had been standing but decided to move downhill. He was moving away from the vehicle and down into a very deep canyon. I was already imagining a tortuous, four-mile pack, all of it uphill … if we got the animal at all!

"Dad, I'll run downslope, get below him, and try to move him back up to you."

"OK, son."

Down I went, bouncing through the spongy parts and jarring through the rocky outcrops. Somehow, I managed to get below the bull. He slowly started to climb back toward Dad's position. The bull passed by Dad about seventy yards away. He expended four more cartridges. They were all misses. The caribou lay down a short distance away. When I got back up to Dad, I was pretty winded.

"What do we do now, son?"

"Do we have any cartridges left?"

"No." We had to put that poor creature out of his and our misery. I got out my sheath knife and approached the bull. He had to be really weak, I reasoned. At ten yards, he stood up. I could have really used one more cartridge!

I decided to make a lasso out of some parachute cord, intending to rope an antler, jerk the bull off his feet, and cut his throat. Amazingly, the loop went over his left antler on the first try. I took a wrap of the cord around my wrist, tightened up the slack, and yanked. Instead of the bull going down, I went flying through the air, landing in a pile of rocks. At least I had enough sense to drop the knife before I hit the ground.

Working some serious kinks out of my arm, I retrieved my knife and readied myself for the next yank. The second yank worked. I stepped in with the knife, and it was over in fifteen seconds.

We were two grown men, one fifty-four, the other twenty-six years old, both shaking, both weeping over the suffering we had caused one caribou. After we got control of ourselves, we butchered the bull, loading the meat into my backpack. I carried the pack and the antlers;

Dad carried the rifle and the hide. On the hike back, he asked me never to tell Mom what a botch we had made of this hunt. I never did.

What went wrong? Back at the vehicle, I discovered that the scope bases were loose. I did not know how that had happened. Ultimately, it was my rifle and my responsibility. In thinking out loud back at the Bronco, I mentioned that the rifle would have to be dropped pretty hard to loosen the bases like that. Dad had a sick look on his face that might have meant that he had, indeed, dropped the rifle while it was out of my sight. But, on the other hand, I had a pretty sick look on my face too.

Bottom line? Check your rifle before and during *every* hunt. Make certain everything is secure and make sure that the rifle is still sighted in properly. That means:

Shoot your rifle before hunting season.
Shoot it before the hunt.
Then you can
trust your sighted rifle.

When my younger son turned eleven, I got him a single-shot, low-recoil hunting rifle. The rifle resembled a miniature Winchester high wall. The cartridge was a .225 Winchester case blown out to shoot .243 caliber bullets. He shot the rifle quite a bit and developed real confidence shooting it. On opening day of caribou season, we spotted a bull about four miles off the road. Out we went, spending part of the afternoon relocating the animal. Once we were close enough, I had the pack down and Jason resting his rifle across it.

We could see the top of the back and the top corner of the lung area at seventy-five yards. The rest of the animal was hidden by willows. We decided he would shoot for the corner of the lungs/spine

area. At the shot, I saw four feet fly up in the air. It was an instant kill. The bullet went exactly where it was aimed.

Several years later, my wife, Marsha, went with Jason and me on a caribou hunt. She had not hunted since she was a girl growing up in Nebraska. I got her a low-recoil, 7-30 Waters single-shot rifle. She shot a caribou at about two hundred yards, holding for a lung shot. It did not drop immediately, running another hundred yards before lying down.

We left Jason with his recently acquired .257 Roberts set up prone over the pack. His instructions were to shoot the bull if he got up and if Marsha and I were well out of the line of fire. Marsha and I headed for the bull in a roundabout path. As we approached from the side, the bull jumped up, moved away, and stopped. Jason shot once, and the bull dropped. His was a perfect lung shot at three hundred yards. Marsha's shot had gone through both shoulders. She did not like the outcome and decided she wanted a bolt-action .243 for caribou, one like she had used as a youngster on deer.

She has now gotten quite a few caribou with that .243. The first was a running broadside shot at thirty-five yards. It happened so quickly that, at the time, I wondered if she would be able to find the animal in the scope. I also wondered if she would be able to keep the rifle swinging as the bull ran. No worries. At the shot, I saw a hole appear right behind the shoulder. She had the next cartridge in the chamber just as the animal started to spray blood with each exhalation.

"Don't shoot! He's lung-shot," I said.

Five seconds later, he was stone dead.

On another hunt, A. J. Paul, his son Oran, Marsha, and I were hunting west of Iliamna Lake. A.J. and I had gotten up early and were hunting quite a way from camp. Two nice bulls appeared, we intercepted them, and we got both. We quickly butchered them and packed up a load of meat. On the way back to camp, we saw a long string of animals on the skyline led by a big bull. They appeared to be near camp.

I said, "I wonder if Marsha and Oran—"

Before I could finish the sentence, the lead bull collapsed. Then we heard the shot. The delay was caused by the distance between the two parties. Instantly, a second bull danced around, ran over a short ridge, and fell down dead. While he was dancing, we heard the second shot.

Marsha hit the first one in the lungs at over two hundred yards; it fell within five seconds. Oran also got a lung shot, but it took a little longer for his bull to fall. We had collected four bulls with four shots, a good morning's work. *Trust your sighted rifle.*

There is more to this story. When the caribou appeared on the skyline above camp, Marsha and Oran were sitting in camp eating Oreo cookies. Oran was wearing long underwear under a regular pair of boxer shorts. Both of them carefully put down the cookies before taking up arms.

We have told friends about this particular caribou hunt, and at least one, a non-hunter, came to the conclusion that we were using the Oreos as caribou bait. Another interesting twist occurred years later when Oran went to a job interview. After answering all of the expected questions, he was faced with one final question: "Are you the one who shoots caribou while wearing only underwear?" Oran admitted to having shot a caribou while clad only in underwear. He got the job.

When Marsha decided she wanted to hunt moose we had to go rifle shopping. Honest. I did not have a rifle that would work well for her since she is right-handed, and I am left-handed. Recoil and weight of rifle were two factors; plus the .243 just is not adequate for moose. She settled on a lightweight 7mm-08 with a three to nine variable scope. It takes her a little while to get the rifle on target so she usually carries it with the scope set to four power. She shoots the rifle really well; I have tried to stay on her good side since she got that rifle.

Her first real moose hunt was a fly-in hunt with Jason, A.J., and me. Neither she nor Jason had ever taken a moose. On the third afternoon of the hunt, Jason got a two-year-old bull. We spent the next day packing moose to the primitive airstrip. The following day, we were shrouded in clouds and blowing snow. It was a tent day.

Jason was still a teenager and did not know about different rifle calibers and external ballistics in nauseating detail. Both A.J. and I did, indeed, know the nauseating details. While Marsha tried to read a book, Jason plied us with questions. What is the minimum caliber for moose? What is the maximum distance for shooting a moose with a .30-06? Is a .30-06 better than a .280 Remington for moose? How much energy is left in a 130-grain .270 bullet at four hundred yards? After literally hours of questions followed by answers and discussions, I learned another critical lesson about hunting: *women do not want to hear about ballistics!* The men decided to find a new subject after Marsha made a thinly veiled comment about loading her rifle inside the tent!

The next morning, we went out to hunt. There was new snow everywhere and a stiff breeze blowing. We started walking, and almost immediately, A.J. spotted another bull heading north across an open meadow. Marsha and I took off to get ahead of it. It would not take long for the bull to pop over a ridge and be gone.

We worked to climb a ridge overlooking the meadow, dodging thickets along a trail of fresh grizzly tracks. Finally, we broke out on top and moved to a spot with a commanding view. Out in the meadow, another two-year-old bull was moving east.

I quickly dropped my pack and arranged it as a shooting rest. Marsha shed her pack and started to lie down behind my pack. I took her rifle and dialed the scope to nine power. The bull was about 325 yards away. As she settled in, the bull was walking broadside. At the shot, I heard the bullet hit. She chambered another round while the bull trotted another 30 yards and stopped.

"Should I shoot again?"

"No, I think he is dead on his feet." I asked, "How did the sight picture look when the rifle went off?"

"Right on the chest, in the lung—" Before she finished the answer, the bull was down. When she put the rifle down, she saw her dead moose way out there. "How far away is that moose?" she asked.

"Right now, it is lying about 350 yards away, "I answered.

"Why did you let me shoot at a moose that far away?"

My response: "*Trust your sighted rifle.*"

A.J. and I used to climb up into the mountains north of Seward to hunt marmots in late summer. We used the hunts to get in shape, tune our shooting skills, collect hides for skin sewing, and lay in a supply of really delicious meat. Actually, I made up that part about delicious meat. We had both hunted tree squirrels in our youths and both had enjoyed eating squirrels. They were delicious. My daughter, Hilary and her older brother Andy had shot red squirrels in interior Alaska when they were children. We cooked and ate them. They were small but delicious. A marmot is just a very large, ground-dwelling squirrel. It should be delicious too, right? Wrong!

I had been encouraged to eat and hunt marmot many years ago. Andy, as a teenager, went caribou hunting with me one fall. We hunted, hiked, and glassed all over the countryside. No caribou. We found a marmot colony on a big rockslide and decided we would not go home empty handed. Andy lay down with the caribou rifle and got three with three shots. All were head shots. He went back to college before we had a chance to eat them. I fried them later, and they were pretty good, definitely better than muskrats.

Armed with that information, A.J. and I were excited. After all, adults are simply bigger, meatier versions of juveniles … we thought. Over several months of marmot hunting, we tried cooking them in a variety of ways: pan fried (very tough, tasted awful), Crock-Potted (tough, tasted awful), pressure cooked (less tough, tasted awful), and ground into burger (somewhat tough, tasted awful) There was no combination of ingredients that made marmot meat worth eating.

However, we had some great days marmot hunting. One morning, we were high on a ridge in a steep canyon, having a snack. I saw a marmot stand up a very long way downslope.

"I have a dollar that says you can't hit it," said A.J.

My response was: "I'll call the shot. Right between the eyes." My .223 rifle was scoped with a good quality 6 to 20 variable. I dialed it up to twenty power. At the shot, the marmot disappeared.

"You missed, Ron."

"I don't think so." Another, or perhaps the same, marmot stood up considerably farther downhill. The distance was pushing three hundred yards. Any bet on this one, A.J.?"

"Not this time, Ron."

"I'll aim for just under the chin," I said. Again, at the shot, the marmot disappeared. We hiked down and found the first one with an entrance hole between the eyes. The second one was hit just below the chin. *Trust your sighted rifle.*

Earlier, I mentioned sighting a scoped rifle to hit point of aim at twenty-five yards. There is a lot to be said for this method. I will give you an example. Years ago in the early fall, Will Barber and I were packing a black bear off a dome in interior Alaska. The previous day, John Fox had shot the bear, and all three of us had shot caribou. We had packed the caribou out to the road, and John had driven them home. Will and I camped out another night and went back for the bear the next morning.

I had just remarked that a mixed bag made for an interesting hunt, when a lone ptarmigan strutted out from among a bunch of boulders. "Hey, Will, maybe we can add ptarmigan to the list!"

"If you shoot it with that rifle the bird will just explode, Ron."

The bird was not spooked so I thought I would try a headshot. Will was highly skeptical and laughing. The rifle was sighted to hit point of aim at twenty-five yards so I laid my pack down twenty-five yards from the bird and settled in for the shot. The bird was standing perfectly still with its neck fully extended. At the rifle report, the bird's head and Will's laugh both disappeared.

Trust your sighted rifle.

13

Shoot a Rifle That Is Comfortable for You

Once again, the title of this chapter gives such obvious guidance that I am embarrassed to write it down. This bit of advice, to me, is in the same category as a household hint I once saw in a magazine: "Too cold in your house? Close the window!" Some things just do not need to be said, right? In this case, wrong.

I wish I had a dollar for every used .338 magnum (or larger) I have seen in Alaskan gun stores. If I could have additional cash for every time I have heard the .338 recommended by a salesperson in a gun store, I would, indeed, be a wealthy man. Here is why there are so many .338s in gun stores.

When cheechako hunters arrive in Alaska, one of the first stops they make is the local gun store. If they are unfamiliar with the Alaskan big-game fauna, they will perhaps ask for advice on choice of rifle caliber. The salesperson recommends a caliber that will be an "all-around" choice, good for everything from Sitka blacktails to large brown bears.

Actually, the .338 is not a bad choice if one really wants a single rifle that will do everything. However, there are two problems with this "all-around rifle" idea. First, many (mostly male) hunters enjoy rifles as interesting mechanical devices, enjoy target shooting, and enjoy hunting a variety of game animals. In other words, they enjoy owning more than one gun. If there really were an "all-around" rifle, there would be no excuse or justification for owning two (or more) rifles. Think about it, men!

Second, an all-around rifle is only suitable for all types of game if it can be shot effectively. Large-caliber rifles such as the .338, .375, .416, and others produce a lot of potentially painful recoil. My supposition about the .338s in gun stores is that neophytes take the salesman's recommendation, buy the .338s, and shoot them poorly because they are so punishing. The ideal, for accuracy, is to hold the rifle steady and slowly squeeze the trigger until the gun discharges. Often, with heavy-recoiling rifles, the shooter flinches and jerks the trigger instead of squeezing it. The shots go all over the place, and the neophyte is hurting and frustrated and, eventually, trades the .338 for something more manageable. Hence, there are a lot of used .338s in gun stores.

Shoot a rifle that is comfortable for you.

Let me state emphatically that I am not suggesting that big bears be hunted with relatively small-caliber rifles. Occasionally, reports appear in Alaska newspapers or hunting magazines about hunters purposely going after brown bears with small-bore rifles such as the .25-06. Such reports almost always make me feel sick to my stomach. The .25-06 is a great cartridge for deer, caribou, sheep, pronghorn antelope, and the like. Typically, 100- to 120-grain bullets are used. These bullets were never designed for and are simply inadequate for large bears unless you intend to and are reliably able to shoot them in the head.

No bear hunter plans to shoot a bear in the head if he/she intends to save the skull. For the purposes of judging for the record books, bears are always scored based on skull measurements. If you blow away part of the skull, you may have no measurement and no possibility of going into the record book, no matter how big the bear.

If you plan to use the bear hide for a rug, a head shot can often produce a large, gaping hole in the head skin. Taxidermists are good, but they cannot work miracles. If you purposely hunt bears, I would not recommend shooting them in the head, though I almost did once.

However, if you are ever compelled to shoot a belligerent bear, you should consider a head shot, especially if you are carrying something short of an elephant gun. If a bear is charging, the head is roughly in the center of what is coming at you. Also, a head shot is the most lethal.

I once asked a very well-known Alaska Peninsula bear guide if he carried a backup rifle.

"Of course. I carry a .243 Winchester," was his reply.

I asked if that was an effective weapon.

"Yeah, kills 'em every time. I shoot 'em in the head." Maybe a 100-grain bullet does not blow too big a hole in the skull of a large brown bear. I hope I never find out.

I have owned four rifles that I considered very adequate for large bears should I run into them. One was a .35 Whelan, two were .405 Winchesters, and the third was a .348 Winchester. One September, a grizzly raided my moose kill before I could finish packing it out. He tore up gear I had left at the kill site and removed the entire hide. I had draped the hide over a downed spruce tree, about twenty-five feet in length. The tree was gone too. Perhaps for spite, the bear left a large pile of poop in the middle of my thoroughly chewed anorak. I decided I needed a "bear stopper."

A few months later, I acquired a bolt action .35 Whelan. The .35 Whelan is a .30-06 blown out to .35 caliber. It seemed like a good idea at the time. That rifle fired 250-grain bullets, almost twice as large as a typical .270 Winchester load. I had a bear rifle! But, I quickly discovered that it would kill on one end and maim on the other. The recoil was simply too punishing for me. After a year or two, I got rid of it. *Shoot a rifle that is comfortable for you.*

I bought my second bear rifle at a Palmer gun show. An old guy from Kodiak had a table at the show, and as I will recount in more detail in the next chapter, he was selling his favorite deer rifle. It was an old, weathered Winchester model 1895 lever action in .405 Winchester. You could, quite literally, kill elephants with this rifle. In fact, Teddy Roosevelt used a model 1895 in .405 on elephants early in the twentieth century.

"Wasn't this a bit of overkill for Kodiak deer?" I asked.

His reply: "Nope. The bullet doesn't mess up much meat, and let me tell you, the bears don't like it!" I purchased a rifle that had been his "all-around" rifle.

Recoil from that .405 is about like several .30-06s I have owned. It is not oppressive. Some of the old 1895s had crescent butt plates and were quite painful to shoot in .405 caliber. Mine has a shotgun-style butt plate and is pretty comfortable. To date, I have bagged a black bear and a snowshoe hare with it. I hit the hare in the head and, therefore, was able to salvage all of the meat. Read the next chapter for the story of the bear and the .405 Winchester. I continue to use the .405 when hunting moose in heavy cover. Bears, moose, and hares? Sounds dangerously close to an all-around rifle!

Years ago, I had a .405 Winchester barrel put on a Browning single-shot rifle. Again, recoil was similar to a .30-06. When I finally got drawn for a Delta bison permit, I decided to take the Browning. Ken Bouwens and I drove down in October and, on the second day of the hunt, crept up on a band of twenty-five. I picked out a two-to-three-year-old bull that was separated from the others. The first shot knocked him off his feet. He could not get up. The .405 was definitely adequate for bison.

To date, I have not used my other bear gun, the .348, on anything except a very large Russian boar and several deer in Texas. It is an original Winchester model 71, lever action. The 200-grain bullets will work well on moose, bears, or anything else in Alaska. The sights are the original iron sights and, therefore, limit the range at which shots should be taken to about 150 yards on moose.

Over the years, I have taken two grizzlies, both with a .30-06. I had Dale Guthrie back me up on the first one. We were hunting bears near Yakutat. One afternoon, we spotted a bear asleep on a bare, rock-strewn exposure on top of a mesa. Within six feet of the bear on every side was head-high brush. One mistake and the bear would dive into the brush and become virtually invisible. We needed the bear to drop immediately. I shot, and then he shot. The bear never got up.

I stumbled on the second grizzly while caribou hunting alone. The bear was feeding on blueberries a half-mile away. At least a half-hour was spent glassing the bear, thinking about the prospects of tackling, perhaps quite literally, a bear by myself. Eventually, I decided to have a go at it and headed for the bear, ever mindful of wind direction. The last one hundred yards took over an hour of crawling, waiting, and crawling again. By the time I set up the shot, I was thirty-five yards away, prone, resting my rifle on my pack. I wanted a broadside lung shot. That would be a lethal hit, and the bear, if I were lucky, would run in the same direction it was facing. When the gun went off, the bear galloped into a big alder patch. I stayed right where I was and recalled the advice I had read years earlier in one of Jack O'Conner's books. He suggested that, in a situation like this, waiting a half-hour without pursuit would give the animal a chance to bleed out and die. I carefully took out my lunch, ate it, and waited another thirty minutes. When I walked into the alder patch, I found the bear dead from a shot through the lungs. Before going down, it ran about thirty yards. By the way, I do not recommend going after bears solo. Too many things can go wrong.

What about moose? Most of my moose have been downed with either a .30-06 or a .270 Winchester. Perhaps the .270, with its 130-grain bullets, is a little light for moose. The .30-06 is a better choice, and if you can shoot them well, the .300 Magnums are even better. Shot placement is critical in big game hunting, and I could shoot that .270 very well. I never lost a moose hit with a .270 or .30-06. My wife uses a 7mm-08 on moose and has bagged one bull with one shot. Years ago, I got a bull with a model 1895 lever action .30-40 Krag.

One of my more interesting moose hunts involved a 12-gauge shotgun. Craig Limpach, a friend who was new to Alaska, wanted to go moose hunting. His only firearm was an old Winchester model 1897 pump shotgun. The design is so old that the gun has a visible hammer. It did not fit into my mental image of a moose gun.

"Do you think this will work on moose?"

I answered, "Yeah, but we will have to get close."

We drove out to a wooded valley and started hiking. We got up high where we could glass down in the bottom and up the other side and started looking. We checked every meadow, clearing, and bush. Then we checked them all again. The tactic is pretty simple. Check out every object that even remotely resembles a moose or a part of a moose. Then, occasionally, recheck all of those objects.

An hour later, I was looking at a brush pile for the tenth time when some of the branches moved. The branches, of course, were the brow tines of a bull moose. We quickly descended, crossed the valley, and approached the bull. I sent Craig straight toward the spot where we had last seen the old boy. I circled to the left, trying to get above the bull.

Eventually, Craig got very close without actually seeing the beast. I was negotiating some chest-high willows and made too much noise. The bull jumped up and ran directly at Craig. It passed by him about fifteen yards away. The 12-gauge slug hit it broadside in the lungs. The impact knocked the old boy over, and he never got up. When we butchered the animal, we found the slug just under the skin on the opposite side from the entry wound. It had expanded to the diameter of a silver dollar. If you are close, the 12-gauge is more than adequate.

Caribou are not hard to kill if hit properly. The list of cartridges that can be used successfully on caribou is a very long one. The ones my family has used include: .243 Winchester, .250 Savage, .257 Roberts, .25-06, .264 Winchester, .270 Winchester, 7mm-08, .280 Remington, .30-40 Krag, .300 Savage, and .30-06.

I have also used three rifles shooting wildcat cartridges on caribou as well. Those were a .30-40 improved 6.5 Krag, and a 6mm-.225, all in single-shot, falling-block rifles. My son Jason shot the 6mm-.225 on his first caribou hunt when he was eleven years old. The rifle produces very little recoil and has an excellent trigger. He got his first caribou with just one shot. The 75-grain Nosler bullet knocked the caribou completely off its feet. All of these cartridges worked well on caribou.

I can think of one final reason to pick a rifle that does not kick too much. I will illustrate my point with a story. Years ago, a husky young Swede named Finn came to the University of Alaska Fairbanks to study wildlife management. He had hunted in Sweden, and he wanted to hunt moose in Alaska. Alaska-Yukon moose are the largest of all moose, far larger than the moose of Scandinavia. He brought a rifle adequate for the largest moose that ever walked, a Swedish Sako chambered for .358 Norma Magnum. The cartridge is an absolute brute, and the rifle kicks like a mule.

Finn arranged a float trip down a northern Alaska river. He took a canoe, his gear, and the .358 Norma Magnum. While floating down the stream, he spotted a huge bull moose. He managed to get out of the canoe and stalk stealthily up to an old blow-down. He used the downed tree as a shooting rest and touched off a shot.

Hours later, Finn awoke blinded and with a terrific headache. At least, he thought he was blind. Actually, he was lying on his back, and his eye sockets were filled with clotted blood. He had snuggled too close to the rifle and had been "scoped." Scoping yourself is easy to do if you get too close to the scope or if the recoil of the rifle is sizeable. Or both.

When he was finally able to remove the clots and get to his feet, he staggered over to see if he'd gotten the bull. He found a very large, very dead moose. Maybe the bull was worth the pain. I don't know.

It is relatively easy to spot shooters who have been scoped because almost all of them have a semicircular scar in or near one eyebrow. I once introduced myself to a stranger and asked him how he managed in life being left-handed like me.

He asked, "How did you know I'm left-handed?"

"Easy. You scoped yourself in the left eyebrow. Therefore, your left eye is dominant."

Shoot a rifle that is comfortable for you.

14

Keep Your Eyes on the Game

It was October 1968. I was fresh out of college and working on my first real job in as a new faculty member at the University of Alaska Fairbanks. I had arrived in Fairbanks with one hunting rifle to my name, a model 1895 Winchester in .30-40 Krag. My dad had lent me one of his rifles as a spare in case I needed one. It was a model 1895 saddle ring carbine in .30-06.

A friend and I had driven up the Steese Highway eager to intercept some Steese-Forty Mile caribou that were reported to be crossing the road. In our naïve minds, we envisioned a vast herd, something like wildebeest on the Serengeti, streaming endlessly past. What could be simpler than just to wait by the road and pick out a nice one? That weekend we did not see very many animals. To up our chances of intercepting caribou, we decided to walk off the road in the direction of the herd. When we found a likely spot, we just sat down and waited. Nothing happened. The title of this lesson and this chapter could easily have been: *learn all you can about your game*.

In reality, a caribou migration is rarely the directed, relentless movement of massive numbers of animals. More typically, smaller bands of three to twenty animals ramble along, alternately walking, grazing, and bedding down for a rest. Not quite the same as wildebeest on the Serengeti plains of Africa.

On the way back to town after this first hunt, I spotted a small band of caribou on top of the ridge at 77 Mile. It was Sunday afternoon, and we decided right then to come back on Tuesday and go after them. Miraculously, when we got there on Tuesday, the caribou were still there. We packed a little gear and some food on our pack frames and started up through the forest.

Thirty caribou, including three decent bulls, were feeding, digging craters through about a foot of crusted snow. My partner Fred (yet another Fred!) and I were lying behind a snow-covered tussock glassing the caribou and the intervening 250 yards of ground. Too far for confident shooting with iron sights and no cover to allow a closer approach. After fifteen minutes, the caribou slowly wandered over a low saddle directly away from us. As the last caribou moved out of sight, we checked our rifles and followed, hoping to get close enough for a shot.

Fred and I approached the saddle and decided to separate by seventy-five yards or so, hoping one or the other would be able to spot the animals in the rolling, willowy terrain. Fred went to the left, and I went to the right. After I lost sight of him, maybe fifteen seconds elapsed before I heard three shots in rapid succession. A single caribou ran out of the brush to my right, about seventy-five yards broadside. My first shot hit it in the lungs; no further shooting was required. Fred had dropped three caribou, including two of the nice bulls, with those three shots. He had filled his limit in about ten seconds! So, the model 95s racked up four caribou with four shots in about thirty seconds that day.

The plan had been to shoot one caribou each. I walked over to Fred and asked why he had decided to shoot three.

"Three? I only wanted one and thought I ended up with two!" he wailed.

When I pointed out the third animal, he looked quite despondent. He should have. We were over a mile from the truck, and the intervening country was mostly a forest of closely spaced black spruce.

But back to my question of Fred: "Why did you shoot three caribou?"

He answered, "I aimed at a bull, shot, and looked down to lever another cartridge into the chamber." When I looked up nothing seemed wounded so I aimed at a caribou and shot. He did not go down either so I levered in another cartridge and looked around for a wounded caribou. I didn't see a caribou staggering so I shot at another caribou, and it fell down."

Basically, every time Fred looked down to work the action on the rifle, a caribou fell down dead. It was pure luck that the third caribou fell down while Fred was still looking. He had two more cartridges in the rifle; we could have ended up with six caribou!

One could draw several conclusions or morals from this story. The first and most obvious is:

Keep your eye on the animal.

You need to know how the animal reacts to your shot and where it goes after the shot. This is such common sense I am embarrassed to write it down.

The second moral to the story is:

Become very familiar with your rifle.

Shoot it ahead of the hunt and, if it has a telescopic sight, sight it in ahead of time. See Chapter 12 for more on sighting in your rifle. Borrowing someone else's rifle is always a risk. In retrospect, Fred or both of us needed supervision. We should have stuck together. Surely, I would have seen the first or second caribou fall down. Hindsight is always great.

We intended to get two caribou. Instead, here we were with four. At least it was entirely downhill to the road ... almost. We set to work and soon had all four animals gutted and propped open. Mine was closest to the road (by maybe a hundred yards) so we decided to pack it out first. Neither of us had ever boned out a game animal so we simply cut the caribou in half. I strapped the back half to my frame; Dean strapped the front half to his. Down the mountain we went. As soon as we got down to the spruce, we discovered that the average distance between spruce trees was less than the span of half a caribou on a pack frame. Every time a leg snagged a tree trunk, we would get spun off balance. The hike resembled a drunken stagger down the mountain. We forded McManus Creek at the bottom and climbed the short distance to the truck. That left three caribou and, meanwhile, the sun was already setting.

Thursday. We would come back Thursday and get the other three.

Fred scrounged up an akio, a fiberglass sled I mentioned in a previous chapter. Since there was a lot of snow on the ground, an akio seemed like a good idea at the time. It weighed thirty pounds without a load. Fred had heard that an akio can move a lot of gear across the snow. We started up the slope by daybreak and spent hours dragging the akio up through the spruce. Breaking out onto the tundra, I could finally see the real application of the akio. We loaded all three whole, gutted caribou onto the sled and started down. When we got down to the forest, we immediately remembered that the width of the akio was greater that the distance between spruce trees. Fighting a fully loaded sled through the trees took hours.

We were exhausted when we finally reached the creek. It was frozen so we slid the akio with our rifles on board across. At least that was the idea. In fact, the sled broke through the ice, and everything went to the bottom of the creek. After fishing the rifles out, we dragged each caribou up the steep hill to the truck. The obvious lesson learned on this part of the hunt was simple:

Learn how to bone out game animals.

This boning lesson was brought home to me years later while hunting caribou on Iowa Ridge, across the Tanana Flats from Fairbanks. Several of us had collected caribou, boned them out, and packed them back to camp. We were relaxing around the tent on a sunny afternoon when another hunter walked over from his campsite about a mile away. We asked if he had had any luck. He said that the only caribou he had seen had been off the top of the ridge, downhill about five hundred feet.

According to him, "It would have taken me a week to drag that caribou up to camp!" Before we could offer instruction about boning out a big game animal, he turned and walked away.

Incidentally, this first caribou hunt was not my last effort with the Model 1895 Winchester. In the spring of 1976, I met a fellow from Kodiak at a gun show in Palmer. He was divesting himself of his deer rifle, a model 95 in .405 Winchester. There are lots of Sitka blacktail deer on Kodiak Island, and they are harvested very effectively with the 300-grain bullet fired from the .405. Bullet construction is sufficiently stout that little meat damage occurs unless you put a round through both hams. In stopping power, the .405 is somewhat under the .375 H&H but is probably superior at close range to the .338 Winchester due to its large bullet diameter.

Aside from little damage to meat, the other, obvious value of the .405 as a Kodiak deer rifle is the potential for dealing effectively with a large Kodiak brown bear. Many deer hunters on Kodiak Island have reported bears showing up within five minutes after shooting a deer. Not only do these bears have an excellent sense of smell, but some also appear to have a conditioned response to a rifle shot. In other words, a rifle shot sounds like a dinner bell to some of these bears. I never pack a Kodiak deer on my back, just in case a bear decides he wants the deer. Instead, I tie a ten- to fifteen-foot rope to the head and the other end to a short stick. With this arrangement, I can simply drag the deer back to the boat, camp, or wherever. All I have to do when a bear shows up is to drop the stick and keep walking. I simply will not argue with a large brown bear over a deer. He or she can have it.

As the old fellow and I talked, I began to realize that he, as much as anything, wanted to find a good home for his rifle. I told him the story of my first caribou hunt, stressing the part about the two model 1895s, and he finally agreed to let me buy it. It came with five boxes of original ammo and four boxes of empty brass plus a handful of solids, suitable for shooting elephants.

That summer, I was out in the garden hoeing, preparing to plant peas in an opening in the woods. We live in the sparsely populated outskirts of Fairbanks with very few neighbors close by. My nearest neighbor, Jim, jogged into the yard and asked if I wanted to shoot a bear.

Since I was pretty wrapped up in gardening at that moment, I replied, "Not particularly. What's up?"

He explained that our next nearest neighbors, the Coadys, had a bear in the yard, the kids were terrified, the dogs were going nuts, and they didn't know what to do.

Since black bears can be hunted year-round in interior Alaska, I ran in the house, grabbed the .405 and a few cartridges, and headed for the Coadys. When we got there, the bear had climbed up a large white spruce tree at the edge of the property and was standing on a branch. The kids were crying, the dogs were still going nuts, and the bear was

also very alarmed. I shot him through the chest, and he dropped so fast that he did not even fall off the branch. Jim offered to climb up and dislodge the bear. While he climbed, I ran home and got the truck. I was able to back it up directly under the branch. When Jim pushed, the bear fell in the bed of the pickup! To date, that was the only time I did not need to lift a game animal into the truck.

However, I nearly repeated this stunt (dropping a game animal *in* the truck) the very next year. It was early summer, and the previous evening, I had loaded garbage bags in the pickup for a morning trip to the landfill. A bad idea when you live in bear country.

At 1:00 AM, our black Lab started barking. He usually slept on the front porch, but the barking was coming from *under* the porch. A sizeable black bear was walking around the house. I grabbed the .405 and tiptoed out the door.

By then, the bear had climbed into the bed of the truck and was ripping open garbage bags. I had the sights on the bear but paused to be sure that the bullet would not hit anything important except the bear. In that instant, the bear sensed me, dove out of the truck, and headed into the woods. He was forty yards from the house when the big bullet caught up to him. I momentarily thought about how much easier it would have been to process the bear if I had dropped him in the bed of the truck. But, forty yards from home was not bad.

The other Winchester 1895 (the .30-40) proved its worth once more in 1997. I was hunting moose in a logging cut west of Fairbanks, calling in the early evening. After an hour of grunts, I heard the brush thrashing of a bull some distance away. Eventually, he walked out into a clearing. My first shot missed completely, but the bull was so obsessed with me as a competitor he just stood there. The second shot put him down. The 220-grain bullet had hit neck and shoulder and had done its job.

I can sum up this chapter easily.

Keep your eye on the game animal.
Learn how to bone out game animals.
Learn about the behavior of the animal you hunt.
Become familiar with your rifle.

Finally, if you can get the bear to fall into the pickup truck, consider yourself lucky!

15

Think Ahead, Plan Ahead, Use Your Head

By now, you realize that forethought, planning, and common sense are really handy for camping, hiking, boating, or hunting in Alaska. Or, anywhere else. You need to give some thought to what you need with you in camp, in your backpack, and on your person. Anyone who has ever gone outdoors in Alaska has certainly done this to some extent. So, in a real sense, this chapter could be considered preaching to the choir.

Consider carrying a backpack at all times. I rarely take my pack off. The stuff in your backpack could, quite literally, save your life. Or, something in your backpack could turn a potentially unsuccessful hunt into a successful one.

What items do you put in your pack before you leave camp? Plan to be gone from camp the entire day and pack accordingly. Raincoat and rain pants are essential for rain and/or wind protection. A fleece jacket or shirt, hat, and gloves may be extremely useful. I also include water purification tablets, a water bottle, matches, insect repellant, small first-aid kit, extra cartridges, flashlight, ace bandage, parachute cord, and either plastic ties or wire closures for trash bags. These last three items are handy for repairing the pack and to attach things to the pack.

Think ahead.

A foil space blanket can be a lifesaver. A lightweight saw can be useful for butchering, antler removal, or cutting firewood … if there IS any firewood to be had. If you do not wear your knife on your belt, it can go in the pack. Do not forget food and, if you butcher your game in the field, include a few game bags and a small tarp. Butchered pieces can be laid on the tarp to keep leaves, mud, and sticks off the meat. Then transfer the pieces to game bags.

Once on a sheep hunt, Dale Guthrie lost the tiny screw that held his glasses together. We fixed it with a garbage-bag wire closure I had in my pack. It was not a very stylish result, but it worked. On another hunt, I lost the clevis pin that held pack to the external frame. I had two extras in my pack and simply replaced the missing pin. Alternatively, the plastic ties used in plumbing and electrical work could hold pack and frame together, attach antlers to a frame, or perform other functions I have not even thought of.

Plan ahead.

Perhaps one of the most obvious functions of a backpack is to carry your game. I realize that, for many, the thought of packing a caribou is not very attractive. Many caribou and moose hunters in Alaska are mechanized to the extent that their ATV, snow machine, or motorized boat does most or all of the actual work. But, even if you use these tools, you may need to go beyond where they can take you. If you drop a caribou a mile away from the machine, do you risk destroying the machine and the tundra? Or, do you cut the beast into packable pieces, put them in or on your pack, and carry them to your transportation?

If the answer is the latter, you will need a pack with enough volume to carry the piece or pieces you have. How much can you carry? You can figure that out with your pack and a bathroom scale before you ever leave home.

Also, get a pack that fits your frame and body build. Do not assume that your pack will fit your spouse or friend. Therefore, lending and borrowing a pack is not the best idea unless you are the same body size as the person lending or borrowing the pack. External frame or internal frame? If you do not already have a pack, go to a sporting goods store that has a variety and try them on. I use an external frame pack with a single, large compartment suitable for carrying an intact caribou hindquarter or two shoulders. My wife, Marsha, has an internal frame pack scaled to her body proportions. Small, zippered compartments on the sides allow us to pack small, essential items that we do not want in the bottom of the large compartment.

During a hunt, I never get much further than three steps from my pack. My life depends on the pack and its contents. In addition, the pack makes a solid shooting rest. The lesson about never leave your pack was engrained in the mind of my son Jason from an early age. When he was thirteen, I sent him with a pack load of meat to the dirt strip on top of Iowa Ridge. He could not figure out exactly where to leave the bag so he left it in his pack and hiked all the way back to camp. I was a little exasperated at the time but also thankful that he had taken to heart the admonition never to leave his pack.

Are you familiar with your hunting area? It is important that you know, generally, the landscape where you hunt. If you have a GPS unit and if it can receive satellite data and if there are GPS maps of your hunting area and if the battery does not run down, fine. If not, you need to have maps of the area and a compass. In addition, it pays to be a careful observer of the landscape in which you find yourself.

Here is an example of how paying attention to your surroundings can be a big help.

One August, many years ago, my previous wife Christine and I went up the Steese Highway to camp the day before caribou season opened. We hiked on the Pinnell Mountain Trail at the Eagle Summit end of the trail. After several miles, we stopped and set up our tent. We would be ready bright and early on opening morning.

In the night, it started raining. Our tent was not the best, and consequently, we woke up wet. A dense fog blanketed the entire area, and we decided to give up and head for the car. With a dense fog, no trail, no map, and no compass, Christine despaired of us getting back.

But, on the way up the trail on the previous day, I had carefully observed the domes and ridges. I remembered the lay of the land and the occasional rock cairns that were the only visible trail markers for much of the way.

"We'll never find our way back," Christine said.

"Yes we will. We will just walk from cairn to cairn, retracing our path from yesterday."

"Which way is the first cairn?"

"That way. Maybe forty yards."

We could not see thirty feet in front of us, so forty yards seemed impossible. However, we walked straight to the cairn.

"OK," she said, "you got lucky on that one. Now what?"

"That direction," I answered. "About fifty yards this time."

"Right!" she said, distrust in her tone.

Fifty yards later, we found the next pile of rocks.

"How are you doing this?"

"I remember the locations of the piles from yesterday. I'm just retracing our steps backward."

In an hour, we were back at our vehicle. Pay attention to the landscape and your path across it. That attention could keep you out of a lot of trouble.

Let us get back to your backpack food. If I had to, I could easily survive for several days on the food that is typically in my pack. It would be Spartan fare, but I would make it. Think about how much energy you burn hiking, climbing, packing heavy loads, or just sitting in a cold wind glassing the landscape.

I try to pack energy-dense food, some of which consists of complex carbohydrates, fats, and proteins. Typically, I walk out of camp with a pound block of cheese, a half-pound of sausage plus crackers, energy bars and/or chocolate bars. Do not forget the water bottle.

In an earlier chapter, I described "defensive eating." Such behavior supplies your body with a more or less continuous energy supply for productive work and a continuous heat supply for staying warm. If, due to unforeseen circumstances, you run out of energy, you can get a quick spike of energy by eating a candy bar. That may tide you over until the cheese, sausage, or ham sandwich kicks in.

Anyone who has ever fed a candy bar to a child has at least one story about how fast the sugar produces a result. Mine involves my son Jason as a five-year-old on a four-mile hike. After the first mile, he was totally out of energy. I had not fed him a sufficiently hardy breakfast, I guess. He was lagging behind his mother, Christine, and me, occasionally complaining that he either a) needed to turn back or b) needed to be carried in the backpack. We gave him a chocolate bar, and within two minutes, he was running up the trail. He ran the remaining mile to the turn-around. Actually, he ran it twice.

Repeatedly, he ran ahead, then walked back to encourage us. Then, he ran ahead again.

"Let's go!"

"We are coming, Jason."

He had no trouble keeping up on the two-mile return.

If you have read this far, you have noticed that my outdoor experiences have not been highly mechanized. I have never owned a snow machine, riverboat, tracked vehicle, Jet Ski, or wheeled, all-terrain vehicle. I do, however, use a four-wheel drive pickup truck to get me to somewhat remote hunting locations. In my early years in Alaska, I drove down mining roads and trails that were, at times, beyond the capabilities of my truck. In short, I got stuck. Repeatedly. Jacking and digging a truck out of a mud-hole is OK, but I would rather be hunting. I thought I had learned a 4WD's limitations, but as recently as the 1990s, I have gotten myself in trouble.

There is more to the story of my caribou hunt the day after running a half marathon. On that day, Paul Matheus and I (that is, I) got my truck mired up to the axles off a mining road trying to get to a nice tent site. Three hours of jacking the vehicle and placing boulders under the wheels did not work. At last, a helpful young man on a four-wheeler came by and towed us out of the mud. I missed three hours of badly needed sleep because I misjudged my truck's capabilities.

Use your head.

Here are two items that I think are highly overrated on outdoor excursions in Alaska: a video camera and a water filtering system. First, the video camera. Lots of hunters now carry video equipment into the field, usually to record the actual kill. That is fine, I guess. But, the moment of the kill is just a small part of the aesthetic of the hunt. Equally important to me are the stalk, the terrain, the weather,

and the salvage of the meat. Still photos serve me well enough. I can describe most of the circumstances from hunts that occurred over forty years ago, and I would rather tell a story to friends than have them stare at a television screen watching the kill.

In addition, a video camera and batteries take up space in your pack that could be used for more essential equipment. And then, if the batteries die, you may miss the *coup de grace*. Let me illustrate the point with a story.

In 2001, Marsha and I hosted and hunted with two friends, Jim Tucker from Wyoming and Mike McGraugh from Illinois. Jim had guided us on pronghorn and mule deer hunts in Wyoming. We all flew into a remote ridge in the foothills of the Alaska Range for a week of moose hunting. Neither had hunted moose previously.

The afternoon before opening day, we spotted two bulls two miles from camp. That night, we went over the gear we would need, including two tarps for butchering and four game bags for packing the first loads of meat back to camp. I gave Marsha the tarp and stuffed two game bags into my pack. I handed the other tarp and bags to Jim. They retired to their tent to organize gear. Marsha and I did the same.

The two-mile stalk went well, and we managed to get within three hundred yards of the two bulls without drawing their attention. A little closer, the cover ran out. Marsha and I positioned ourselves on a high point, hidden by willows. Jim and Mike crawled down a low gully angling towards the bulls. Jim left his video camera with us, and we were to film the stalk and the shots.

Soon, the bulls began to either hear or smell Jim and Mike. They turned toward the hunters and began to shift their weight nervously. I moaned a loud cow vocalization, and both bulls turned to face us. For the next fifteen minutes, the two animals alternated between facing in the direction of Mike and Jim when they made noise and facing us when I cut loose with another cow moan.

Finally, our friends got into position. I raised the camera and pressed the trigger. It started filming but ground to a halt within five seconds. Dead battery. No spare. Then, the shooting started, and very quickly, both moose were on the ground.

After the congratulations and a multitude of photos, we rolled up our sleeves. When both bulls were gutted, I asked Jim to get out his tarp and game bags. He instantly looked embarrassed.

"I didn't bring them, Ron."

"Why not?"

"They wouldn't fit in my pack." Of course, the video camera had displaced the tarp and game bags. By not having the game bags, we made two extra four-mile round trips to camp. By the way, those two bulls, one with a sixty-seven-inch rack and the other with a fifty-inch, required twenty game bags, each of which contained over fifty pounds of boneless meat. That is the equivalent of one person packing fifty pounds over a distance of forty miles.

Think ahead.

Packing those moose back to camp required six days of effort. Fortunately, the weather was cool, and we did not lose any meat. At least, we did not lose any meat to spoilage. We did lose one bag that was carried off by a grizzly.

During the packing, Jim and Mike came to realize how tough Marsha is. She packed fifty-pound loads, day after day, over really awful terrain including tussock bogs, streams, and steep uphill and downhill stretches. The three of us were amazed at Mike's determination. He is a Vietnam War veteran who, during the conflict, stepped on a mine and lost parts of his lower legs. Pain is a constant in his life, but he never complained about the hard work of packing. It was an honor to help him bag a moose and get it back to camp.

Now, I will say something about the water filtration system I mentioned earlier. Jim had one in his backpack too. This is the other item I find highly overrated. In Alaska, a hunter's source of drinking water is often ponds on the tundra or in bogs. These ponds usually have a lot of particles of organic matter. This stuff quickly clogs many of these filters. Rather than worry with a clogged filter, I either boil the water or add purification tablets. If you do not like the taste of iodine, carry some powdered drink mix to mask the flavor. Powdered lemonade or iced tea work great.

Plan ahead.

A potentially useful piece of equipment in Alaska's outdoors is a satellite phone. I have never used one but understand how they could save your life in a desperate situation. Here is a caution: do not use the presence of a satellite phone as an excuse to take foolish risks. If you have read this far, you are probably thinking, "Look who is talking about taking foolish risks!" Similarly, I have taken foolish risks driving and gotten stuck BECAUSE I had a four-wheel drive vehicle.

Believe me, I KNOW how the foolish mind works. Something like this: "I think I'll jump that too-wide, boulder-filled stream. After all, if I break my leg, I can always use my satellite phone to call for help."

Use your head.

A piece of equipment I never intend to use for hunting in Alaska is a bicycle. As teen-agers growing up in the California desert, my brother, Rob, and I took our bicycles and went quail hunting several times. No, we did not try to shoot while pedaling. Instead, we just used the bikes to get us up in the hills. Our shotguns were tied to the frames of our bikes. We each rode with a daypack containing water, lunch, and shotgun shells. One day on our way to the hills, we were stopped by a California Highway Patrolman. We explained what we were doing, and he asked us to be careful. He neglected to tell us that we were violating a law prohibiting minors from carrying firearms without an accompanying adult. I learned about this law at midnight in an alfalfa field three years later. But, that is another story.

Bicycles are occasionally used by Alaskan hunters. I had an acquaintance in Seward who was an avid hunter and an avid mountain biker. One year, he got drawn for a caribou permit on the Kenai Peninsula and decided to bike up the Resurrection Pass trail.

He was successful in bagging a caribou, but on the way down, he lost control, pedaled off the trail, and banged himself up. I cannot imagine maintaining enough dexterity and balance while carrying a boned-out caribou in a backpack on a bike. Even putting some of the weight in bike saddlebags would not alleviate the problem for me. I will leave the bicycle hunting to the really tough, hardcore mountain bikers.

Previously, I mentioned tents and tent sites. Perfectly flat sites near water and completely out of the wind are great. Bring bug spray. However, I have camped where there were no flat spots for a mile. We camped near a ridge top once and had to walk over four hundred yards to the nearest water. We have pitched tents near ridge tops and had the wind blow the tent flat while we were in it. Moving a tent to a more favorable location in a high wind is no fun. It is better to try to get it out of the wind in the first place. On several hunts, we have sawed our way into the middle of an alder thicket to get protection from the wind. *Think ahead* and look for protection from the wind.

The size of the tent depends, mostly, on how far you have to carry it. A lightweight mountain tent is about all the weight you can afford on a sheep hunt. If you are dropped off by boat or plane and plan to stay in one campsite, you can use a bigger, more comfortable tent. On all but the most Spartan hunts, take a backup tent. If one tent fails, you still have another tent. If a bear rips through one tent, you still have another. If he tears up both tents, you need to seriously consider camping out under his stretched hide.

Marsha asked me to mention sleeping bags in this chapter. The first time we went on a hunting trip together, I lent her one of my better sleeping bags. She could not get warm in that bag. I bought a fleece liner for the bag, but that was not enough. She was still cold. The next summer, we went to Kearny, Nebraska, for her high school reunion and stopped in a Cabela's outlet. She spied the sleeping bags and picked out a bag that was rated to -30°. In terms of warmth, it was the perfect bag for her on late summer/early fall hunts. I think the bag weighs eight pounds. It definitely is not a backpacking bag. But, she stays warm at night. Be sure you have enough bag to meet your (or your wife's) needs.

No matter how much you have camped, hunted, or read about these outdoor activities, there will always be novel situations to confront. In spite of all the planning ahead and thinking ahead, at some point you will have to *use your head*, your common sense. Do not leave it at home.

Try to stay down to earth in your planning. If your idea sounds like a crazy idea to your friends, there is a high probability that it is, indeed, a crazy idea. Of course, I have an example, and surprisingly, it does not involve me!

Many years ago, Dale Guthrie regularly went sheep hunting with an engineer, a fellow who was always coming up with bright ideas to save himself time and effort. Dale and his friend hunted the same location for several years, and both bagged sheep. The pack back to the airstrip always led to a very steep scree slope with loose rocks that shifted under their feet. With one-hundred-pound packs, they had to negotiate the slope slowly and carefully.

Dale's friend (I'll call him Fred, but he is a different Fred, not the previous Freds) put his mind to the problem and came up with a solution. Fred sewed a heavy canvas bag that he could load with the sheep meat. When they got to the dreaded slope, Dale started picking his way down as usual. Fred, on the other hand, stopped and transferred his sheep meat to his prized canvas meat bag and, after yelling a "MEAT BAG!" warning to Dale, pushed it down the slope.

The bag began tumbling, picking up speed. On the third bounce off the rocks, the meat bag experienced a "materials failure." That is, the bag ripped open. Instead of one meat bag hurtling downslope, there were dozens of meats flying helter-skelter. None of the individual projectiles made it as far as the bottom of the slope. In fact, no two pieces landed in the same spot.

It took Fred hours to retrieve his meat and pick off the major pieces of filth. What should have taken an hour, instead, took three hours.

Use your head.

Just because you have a thought in your head, it does not mean that the thought is real … or intelligent.

In summary, as you prepare for and execute your Alaskan hunt:

- Think about water and lightning.
- Don't overestimate your transportation, especially if YOU are the transportation.
- Keep your canoe upright and try really hard not to poke holes in the bottom.
- Try to keep your sweating to a minimum. If you do get really sweaty, for heaven's sake, don't get yourself frozen to a road!
- Check which way the wind is blowing.
- Get in good condition and try not to overdo it just before the big hunt.
- Remember, sometimes you can't get back to camp.
- Keep track of your knife.
- Have plenty of food with you.
- Hunt right up to the end.
- Decide who is going to shoot.
- Trust your sighted rifle.
- Make sure you can handle the recoil of your firearm.
- Keep track of the animal you shoot.
- Above all, use your head!

I hope you do not make ALL the mistakes I have made. But, I also hope that you enjoy the outdoors and hunting as much as I have. Good luck. I'm rooting for you.

About the Author

Ronald Smith is an emeritus professor of biology at the University of Alaska Fairbanks. He retired after thirty-one years of teaching and research in Alaska. He is the author of forty-four scientific papers, most of which are about Alaskan animals, and the book, *Interior and Northern Alaska: A Natural History*. He and his wife, Marsha, divide their time between interior Alaska and the Hill Country of Texas.

About the Cartoonist

Jeanne Mars Armstrong is a retired educator who creates cartoons and paintings in her home studio. She and her husband, Michael, live in a log home on a ridge just outside Fairbanks, Alaska. With no local family, they fill their daily lives with dear friends, beloved pets, and terrific adventures in the wilds of Alaska.